AMUNDSEN OF THE ARCTICS

⌘

C.H. COLMAN

Copyright © 2011 C.H. Colman
All rights reserved. Including the right of reproduction in whole or in part in any form.

ISBN: 1461120357
ISBN-13: 978-1461120353
LCCN: 2011909082

Library of Congress Cataloguing-in-Publication Data
Colman, C.H.
Amundsen of the Arctics/ C.H. Colman
Summary: "A biography of the Norwegian explorer Roald Amundsen. Tells how Amundsen discovered the Northwest Passage, was first at the South Pole, and made the first crossing by air of the North Polar Basin. Includes a bibliography, source notes, as well as an index. "
Juvenile literature.

Printed in the United States of America by CreateSpace
www.createspace.com
Display type set in Requiem HTS Roman
Text type set in New Baskerville Roman

Contact Author: mail@chcolman.com

Fancourt Publications
2754 Linshaw Court
Cincinnati, Ohio 45208

To my wife, Pamela, who encouraged me in the writing of this book
– C. H. C.

Contents

Foreword vii

The World in 1872 1

Amundsen's Early Years 7

Crossing Hardangervidda 15

First Person to Ski and Sled in the Antarctic 23

The Northwest Passage Part One 33

The Northwest Passage Part Two 45

Planning for the North Pole 59

Heading to the South Pole 73

Preparing to Leave for the Pole 81

Crossing the Great Ice Barrier 93

Through the Mountains 101

The Race to the South Pole 111

Scott 119

The Return 129

The Years Fly By 139

Farewell 155

Epilogue 161

Foreword

Cast yourself back to the age of Arctic exploration, when men like Peary, Cook, Scott, and Shackleton were striving to reach the Poles. Perhaps the greatest explorer of them all, the "Napoleon of the Polar regions," was the Norwegian, Roald Amundsen.

Amundsen was a different type of leader. He brought an unmatched professionalism to the science of exploration in addition to being a natural motivator. He was fearless and open to learning from other cultures. He was also a practical man. It was hard for him to lie, but he did so on at least two occasions when he felt deception was justified. He loved animals, yet he made the difficult decision on one expedition to kill most of his huskies.

The British criticized Amundsen and misrepresented his achievements. Americans loved Amundsen and provided much of his money by paying for lecture tours or making donations. President Theodore Roosevelt wrote to Amundsen after each of two expeditions.

Who was the real Amundsen? Was he as underhanded as the British made out? Or was he a hero as most Americans believed?

I

THE WORLD
IN 1872

On July 16, 1872, Roald Amundsen (Roh-ahl Ah-moon-suhn) was born into a world where horses pulled carriages and gas lamps lit streets. The Great Chicago Fire had finished burning only a few months previous, while George Armstrong Custer had yet to make his last stand. Parts of the planet were undiscovered. No one had stood on the ice that covered the ocean over the North Pole. No one had explored the coldest continent, Antarctica, yet alone reached the South Pole. And, although sailors had dreamed of it since Columbus reached America, no one had sailed through the Northwest Passage from the Atlantic Ocean to the Pacific Ocean, around the top of Canada.

Amundsen grew up in Norway, a country where lakes froze and snow filled valleys. Ponies wore snowshoes to step through drifts, while men and women glided on skis or sleighs. Roald's home town of Borge was near what is now Oslo, Norway's capital city, to which the Amundsens moved when Roald was three months old. In 1872, Oslo was called Christiana, and Sweden ruled Norway. Many Norwegians wanted to govern their own country.

Norwegians had been explorers since their Viking days. A thousand years before the birth of Roald Amundsen, Eric the Red started the first settlement in Greenland, the world's largest island, which lies between Canada and Norway. Eric the Red's son, Leif Ericson, may have been the first European to reach North America, setting out from Greenland and surfing his long ship down waves until he reached a place he called "Vinland."

Amundsen in 1875

At the time Roald Amundsen was born, Norwegians were using their knowledge of snow and ice to explore the Arctic regions north of their country.

An Arctic explorer is what Amundsen wanted to be. Looking back on his life, he said, "How did I happen to become an explorer? It did not just happen, for my career has been a steady progress toward a definite goal since I was fifteen years of age. Whatever I have accomplished in exploration has been the result of lifelong planning, painstaking preparation, and the hardest kind of conscientious work."

2
Amundsen's
Early Years

Roald's father was a captain and ship owner. Roald's mother took care of her four sons during the months that her husband was away. Roald grew up in a world of the sea and of the snow. He learned in his father's shipyard about building hulls for storm waves. In winter, Roald strapped on skis and glided down the snow-covered road outside the garden gate. He wore skates to skim across sea ice to nearby islands

When Roald was fourteen, his father died at sea. The three older sons left home to find work, while Roald stayed with his mother, who wanted him to become a doctor.

At the age of fifteen, Roald read the writings of Sir John Franklin, the English explorer who died in 1847 while trying to find the Northwest Passage. The thought of being trapped in ice didn't scare Roald. Nor did it scare him that Franklin became so hungry when returning from one of his expeditions that he ate animal bones at a deserted Indian camp, and then ate boot leather. These were sufferings that Roald wanted to experience. "Strangely enough the thing in Sir John's narrative that appealed to me most strongly was the sufferings he and his men endured. A strange ambition burned within me to endure those same sufferings. Perhaps the idealism of youth, which often takes a turn toward martyrdom, found its crusade in me in the form of Arctic exploration. I, too, would suffer in a cause…in the frozen North on the way to new knowledge in the unpierced unknown. In any event, Sir John's descriptions decided me upon my career. Secretly, because I would never have dared to mention the idea to my mother, who

I knew would be unsympathetic, I irretrievably decided to be an Arctic explorer."

Roald kept his bedroom window open at night so he could practice sleeping in cold weather. When his mother became anxious about his health, Amundsen explained to her that he liked fresh air. Whenever he had time off from school, he took ski trips exploring the nearby hills and mountains.

The same year that Roald learned about John Franklin, a Norwegian who would become a lifelong supporter of Amundsen, Fridtjof Nansen (Frit-yof Nan-suhn) made the first crossing of the "huge glass mountain" that is Greenland. He and five companions sailed to the Greenland Sea, clambered from their ship into a small boat, and rowed into the ice. They traveled for twelve days, pitching their tents on floes and jumping back into their boat when waves hammered the ice. They reached shore, put on snowshoes, and pulled their sleds into the mountains. They changed their snowshoes for skis, climbed to the ice-covered plateau, and began the crossing.

Each night, reindeer-skin sleeping bags kept them warm. It took six weeks to reach the other coast of Greenland. In 1889, Nansen returned as a hero to Christiana, sailing up the fjord in an armada of boats. Amundsen, still at school, was among the cheering crowds that welcomed Nansen back.

Roald entered Christiana University to study medicine. He still wanted to become an explorer, and so he skied through nearby forests to learn how to live in cold weather. In 1893, a Norwegian called Eivind Astrup came to speak at the University. Astrup had traveled in northern Greenland with the American explorer Robert Peary. Astrup inspired Amundsen by talking about how the Inuit survived cold, something that British explorers like John Franklin had ignored because they thought that wool clothing and tinned food were better than anything primitive peoples might use. Astrup said Inuit animal fur clothing was warmer than wool, eating lots of fresh meat prevented disease and maintained strength, learning to build an igloo provided a warm place to sleep in deep cold, and most important that dogsleds and skis were the fastest way to move across snow. Amundsen never forgot these lessons.

THE CARAVAN ON THE MARCH. (By A. Bloch, from a photograph.)

Nansen Crossing Greenland

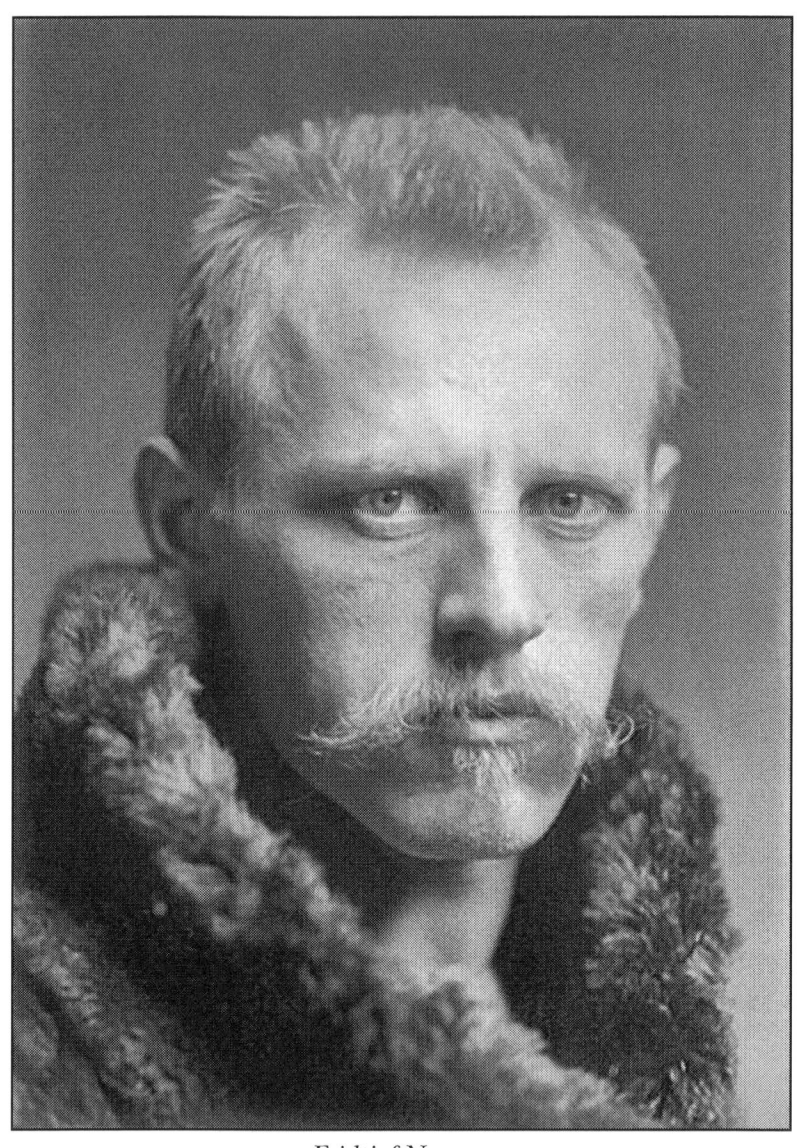

Fridtjof Nansen

Roald did poorly in medical school. He did not tell his mother. "Like all fond mothers, mine believed that I was a paragon of industry, but the truth is that I was a worse than indifferent student. Her death two years later, in my twenty-first year, saved her from the sad discovery which she otherwise would have made, that my own ambitions lay in another direction and that I had made poor progress in realizing hers. With enormous relief, I soon left the university, to throw myself whole-heartedly into the dream of my life."

Roald had actually failed his medical exams in June, 1893, three months before his mother's death.

He wrote letters to explorers, one of whom replied that he only took people he knew and told Amundsen that he should learn to train and care for dogs because they would be useful on any trip to the Arctic.

Astrup had already convinced Roald about dogs, but since there were few huskies in Norway, it was difficult for Amundsen to learn how to dogsled. He kept on practicing his skiing instead.

3
CROSSING
HARDANGERVIDDA

Amundsen's mother is remembered as saying that her son, Roald, was the last of the Vikings. He stood over six feet tall, with fair hair, blue eyes, and a nose that made him look like an eagle.

Roald wanted to learn from the past. He read all the books he could get on Arctic exploration so as not to repeat mistakes. Most of these expeditions required ship travel. Amundsen found that troubles developed when the leader of an expedition wanted to do things that a ship's captain disagreed with. Amundsen decided that he would never lead an expedition unless he could also be in charge of the ship. In 1894, Roald began training to become a captain. He signed on aboard a sealing ship and sailed into the Arctic to hunt seals for their skins and the oil in their fat. Amundsen learned a lot about sailing, but didn't like sealing because so many animals were killed.

Upon returning to Norway from the sealing voyage, Amundsen sailed on one of his family's ships and passed his exam to become a ship's officer, called a "first mate." He was making good progress towards becoming a captain, but had to stop for seven months to complete his military service, a government requirement of all young men.

Amundsen was near-sighted, a state of vision that he said gradually improved over his life. Still, his eyesight would have stopped him from entering military service, and that mark on Roald's record might have led expedition leaders to choose other explorers. Amundsen had to take an army physical examination. As he tells it, "I was ushered into an office where the chief examiner sat behind a desk with two assistants. He was an elderly physician, and, as I quickly discovered, to my extreme embarrassment, an enthusiastic student of the human body. I was, of course, stripped to the skin for the examination. The old doctor looked me over and at once burst into loud exclamations over my physical development. Evidently my eight years of conscientious exercise had not been without their effect. He said to me: "Young man, how in the world did you ever develop such a splendid set of muscles?" I explained that I had always been fond of exercise…So delighted was the old gentleman at his discovery…that he called to a group of officers in the adjoining room to come in and view the novelty…the good old doctor entirely forgot to examine my eyes."

Military service involved a lot of parade ground marching, which bored Roald, but he liked his sergeant, Peter Ristvedt. They stayed in touch and would work together again.

In January 1896, Amundsen and his brother Leon used their holiday time to set out on an expedition. Near Christiana, a line of mountains rises to the largest plateau in Europe, called Hardangervidda, which stretches seventy miles to the coast of Norway. In summertime, herdsmen tended their reindeer on the plateau, but deep snow prevented anyone from crossing the area in winter. It was a trip which Amundsen said "involved dangers and hardships fully as severe as any…in the polar regions."

Roald and his brother decided to make the first winter crossing of Hardangervidda, from a farm called Mogen on the side of the plateau near Christiana to a farm called Garen on the other side at the coast. The brothers wanted to travel light, so they took no tent. Wrapped inside their reindeer skin sleeping bags were two lamps and some food: crackers, chocolate, and butter. They had a map and three compasses which, with his seaman's training, Roald knew how to use. Strapping on their skis, Roald and Leon glided across the snow until they found Mogen farm in a valley below the plateau. Six people lived in the one-room house: an old man, his wife, and two sons with their wives. This family welcomed Roald and Leon, who spent the night in front of the fireplace. A blizzard kept them inside the farmhouse for eight more days. The old man said that crossing the plateau was too dangerous, but showed the brothers the best place to start. Roald thought the expedition would be simple. He knew how to ski and would complete the trip in two days.

The first day Roald aimed for a hut halfway across the plateau. Sunlight didn't last long in the Norwegian winter, but the brothers reached the hut that evening. Nails held the door and window shut, while heavy boards covered the chimney. The temperature was ten degrees below zero Fahrenheit. By the time they had climbed the roof and opened the hut, their fingers had lost feeling. Inside, wood lay stacked beside the fireplace, but cold air coming down the chimney pushed smoke into the room as the brothers tried to start a fire. Tears streamed from their eyes before the flames shot up.

In the morning, wind slammed snow into the sides of the hut. The storm kept Roald and Leon inside for two days. They found a bag of flour, and cooked porridge in an iron pot because they wanted to save the food in their bags.

On the third day, the storm weakened. The brothers decided to ski the last half of the trip to Garen farm. They checked the compass and set out.

The temperature rose, and snow fell; large, wet flakes melted on their map each time they opened it. Finally they had to throw it away. Night overtook them before they reached the edge of the plateau. The brothers unrolled their sleeping bags, took out the food bags, and stuck them by their feet. They marked the food bags with their ski poles in case snow covered them, and climbed into the reindeer skins. Their clothes steamed. The temperature dropped. Teeth chattering, the brothers fell asleep. Roald woke hungry in the darkness. He clawed for his food bag, but found only snow beside his ski pole. At daybreak the brothers still couldn't find the bags, which had perhaps been taken by an animal.

They headed toward the coast in a snowstorm so heavy that they could only see as far as their ski tips. Roald's compass didn't help because he didn't know where he was when he pointed it. The brothers decided that with such bad weather they shouldn't go near the cliffs along the coast, so they turned back for the hut in the middle of the plateau. They wandered lost for days without food, sleeping in the open, and getting weaker. Roald was suffering like the explorer John Franklin.

On the fourth night, the brothers reached the slope of a small peak and settled down out of the wind. Leon climbed into his sleeping bag. Roald dug into the snow and made himself a cave not much larger than his body. He climbed in head first and pulled his bag in behind him. In the middle of the night he woke lying on his back with his right wrist across his eyes. Roald couldn't move because the wet snow had frozen around his body. He shouted to Leon, then stopped because he knew he would run out of air. He fell asleep again and woke to faint sounds and tugging on his boots. Leon took three hours to dig his brother out.

Leon explained that the only reason he had not also scooped out a cave was that he was too tired. Had he done so, the brothers would have died.

Roald set a course by the stars. Although the brothers had cracked ice to find water in small streams, they had not eaten for four days. It was difficult to move one ski ahead of the other. They pushed through deep snow until Leon disappeared.

Roald threw himself on the ground and yelled.

Leon shouted that he had fallen over a precipice. His sleeping bag had saved him when he dropped thirty-feet and landed on his back. Roald scrambled down, and the brothers waited until it was light. They found ski tracks leading to a shed, stumbled inside, and crawled under straw. The next morning, they followed those tracks to the Mogen farmhouse, from which they had started the crossing of Hardangervidda.

They had skied in circles.

Meanwhile, near the coast, a farmer found ski tracks coming from the middle of the plateau. The brothers had turned back just a few feet from the cliffs at the edge of the plateau.

The crossing of Hardangervidda almost killed Amundsen, but his mistakes taught him to make better plans. He and Leon had gone around in circles, like people often do when they are lost. Even with compasses, they hadn't known when they reached the coast. In the future, Roald would take better maps and navigational equipment. He would pack more food and make wiser judgments about when to continue a journey. It had been risky leaving the midway hut. He and Leon should have returned to it when it started snowing.

4

FIRST PERSON TO SKI
AND SLED IN THE ANTARCTIC

When Roald Amundsen had finished his army training he searched for the next way to realize his dream of becoming an Arctic explorer. He wanted to join an expedition where he could get the experience necessary to become a licensed captain, while also exploring an Arctic region. There were no explorers in Norway who needed Amundsen at that time, so he applied to join the Belgian Antarctic Expedition led by a naval officer called Adrian de Gerlache. This expedition was interested in magnetism, a major area of scientific inquiry in the 1800s.

Magnetism is the force around a material that pulls or pushes another material, like when a magnet sticks to a refrigerator door. Electric currents in the Earth's liquid core create a magnetic force field around the planet. This magnetic field extends thousands of miles into space and has two "Magnetic Poles," where the force points straight down into the center of the planet. In Amundsen's time, these Magnetic Poles were known to be somewhere in the north and south of the planet, but located hundreds of miles from the geographical top and bottom, which are called the "North Pole" and the "South Pole." Adrian de Gerlache wanted to reach the South Magnetic Pole. He liked the fact that Amundsen was both an experienced sailor and a skier, so he offered him a job as an officer: the position of second mate.

The objective of finding the South Magnetic Pole was soon abandoned for want of time and money, but de Gerlache intended to make discoveries for the Belgian Government: by drawing maps, recording weather patterns, and taking magnetic measurements. He also wanted to become the first man to spend a winter in Antarctica.

Adrian de Gerlache

De Gerlache's ship, *Belgica*, was a Norwegian sealing vessel built for high waves and ice. Amundsen was supervising preparations one day when a square-faced Norwegian walked past the "Admittance Forbidden" sign and asked if he could see over the ship. Helmer Hanssen remembered, "I simply had to see this ship, which was going on a voyage of adventure to the Ant-Arctic...and asked for permission to go on board. I was told I would have to ask the Mate...I told him I wanted to see over the ship. He said I could and went with me and showed me everywhere. From the first minute I took a liking to this big fine-looking man with the kind face. I thanked him, and then I separated from Roald Amundsen. He went south and I went north."

The two men would meet again.

The *Belgica* expedition set sail in the summer of 1897. An American, Frederick Cook, was the ship's doctor. He, like Astrup, had traveled with Robert Peary in Greenland, so Roald was interested in learning all he could from Cook about life in the Arctic.

In January, 1898, the *Belgica* reached the continent of Antarctica and sailed along the coast. It was summertime in the Southern

Hemisphere. Although deep snow remained on land, some parts of the shore were free of ice. The expedition discovered a long channel now called the Gerlache Strait, and explored several islands, taking measurements. On one of these islands Amundsen probably became the first person to use skis in Antarctica.

Belgica in front of Mount William

The *Belgica* recorded ocean depths and stopped at Brabant Island, northwest of Mount William along the Gerlache Strait. Amundsen, Dr. Cook, and some others made a one-week sledding journey to the top of the island in order to map the Strait. Amundsen learned several things from this trip during which, for the first time, sleds were used in the Antarctic. Amundsen found it difficult to haul a heavy load without dogs, and he sweated into woolen clothes. Dr. Cook explained that his sealskins were warmer and dryer than wool. Finally, Amundsen learned the difficulties of camping in a windy place. He wrote that his tent "presents too great a surface to the wind. It is made of oiled silk…not practical…heavier than untreated material. The most practical form…is undoubtedly the conical. It is easier to pitch and doesn't offer so much wind resistance." In the future, Amundsen would use a tent that only had one pole so that it could be raised quickly.

The *Belgica* upped anchor, left the island, and sailed into a sea of icebergs which had "calved" or split away from the ice that covered the land. A gale was blowing one afternoon when Second Mate Amundsen took over steering the ship. Wind whipped spray into his face. Captain Gerlache pointed to an iceberg that had been protecting *Belgica* from the biggest waves and told Amundsen to stay close to the giant. Roald did so all afternoon and evening, then turned over the command, went below, climbed into his bunk, and fell asleep. He awoke to find the ship as still as if it were anchored in a harbor. Roald pulled on his clothes and rushed up to the deck. Walls of ice towered above *Belgica*, which floated on a pool of flat water. Outside, the sea foamed. In the night, a wave had pushed *Belgica* into a space between two icebergs. Knowing that the bergs could break at any minute, the captain steered over underwater ice and back into the ocean.

Another storm roared down from the north and hammered the ship, pushing it toward a field of ice that stretched for miles. Captain de Gerlache and his first officer spotted an opening and turned toward it, trying to escape being shipwrecked. Amundsen believed that *Belgica* could still have clawed into the storm and away from the ice field, but he did not say this because his two senior officers had made their decision. The wind howled as the *Belgica* surfed over waves. The ship scudded between ice floes. The waves died in the frozen waste. Ice closed in and trapped the ship.

Although the captain tried to steer out of the ice pack, he did not succeed. His men believed that de Gerlache had wanted the ship to become trapped so that he might, perhaps, drift with the ice further into the Antarctic than any person before him. The second in command, Lieutenant Lecointe, wrote "It is certain that we honestly tried to return northwards, but it is also certain that de Gerlache and myself were happy at the failure of our attempt."

Belgica in Ice

The original plan had been to establish a winter land camp for Captain de Gerlache and three men while *Belgica* returned to a warm water port. It was dangerous to leave a vessel in the Antarctic because ice could crush the hull or trap the ship for years.

The sun dropped below the horizon and stayed there.

The Antarctic night had arrived.

The men shivered. They wondered if they would ever get out of their trap. They were angry with their captain, and because they had no fresh food, scurvy made them sick. Their mouths got sore. Their gums became soft as sponge and turned from whitish-pink to purple. Their teeth loosened. Dark spots appeared on their legs. Old wounds throbbed while legs and arms swelled. The skin behind their knees turned black.

Although many scientists thought that people caught scurvy like they caught a cold, both Amundsen and Dr. Cook believed from their reading of Arctic travels that eating fresh meat prevented scurvy. The two men went onto the ice and killed seals and penguins, which they dragged back to the ship. Unfortunately Captain de Gerlache didn't believe in the value of fresh meat and forbade any of his crew to eat seal or penguin.

Scurvy made the captain and his lieutenant even sicker. They stayed in their bunks. Amundsen, his hair turning grey at the age of 26, took over command. He ordered the cook to serve fresh seal and penguin meat, preserving the vitamins by not overcooking. Everyone, including Captain de Gerlache, was hungry enough to eat what was served. Amundsen wrote, "Within a week, all the men plainly showed an improvement in their condition."

Amundsen spent many hours talking with Dr. Cook about better ways to explore the Arctic and Antarctic. They discussed food, clothing, sleeping bags, tents, sleds, and skis. Just as Franklin's suffering had attracted Amundsen, his own suffering on the *Belgica* fascinated him. He made notes about how he and the crew reacted to scurvy, relishing in the chance to experience what he had only read about.

Ice had held *Belgica's* hull for five months by the time the sun rose into the horizon's orange glow. The expedition had become the first to spend a winter in the Antarctic. The men did not want to become the first to also die there.

Belgica had been trapped for nearly a year by the time Christmas arrived during the Antarctic summer. A basin of water formed a mile from the ship. Dr. Cook thought that the ice pack would break up and make a channel to the sea. The *London Times* reported (June 25, 1901) "Until December the members of the expedition had every confidence that the sun would melt the ice and break up the floes, but when that month was passed they began to feel deceived, and resolved to attack the encircling floe with explosives. The result was imposing as a spectacle, but no fracture was made in the ice, so they began to cut a channel, 700 metres long and wide enough for the ship to pass, through the floe along an old fracture where the ice was only 1.6 to 1.9 metres thick. Finally, after a month's work day and night the Belgica, aided by a storm, was freed…"

The day the waterway reached the basin, the Belgica crew went to bed planning to sail their ship into its new harbor.

Overnight, the ice shifted and closed the channel.

The next day the wind changed, and the channel opened up again. *Belgica* started her engines and glided into the basin, where she waited for weeks. Finally, thirteen months after the decision to sail away from the storm and into the ice field, a lane cleared from the basin to the sea. *Belgica* started its engines, got underway, and became stuck between two icebergs that towered above her decks like mountains. Dr. Cook made sealskin mats and hung them over the sides to shield the hull from the ice. Several days later, the ice parted and *Belgica* floated into open water.

Amundsen returned to Europe in 1899 after two years of Antarctic schooling. He refrained from criticizing de Gerlache, commenting some years later about the decision to enter the ice pack, "Gerlache knew for a certainty that unless he returned with results that would please the public, he might just as well never return at all. Then the thickly packed ice opened, and long channels appeared, leading as far southward as the eye could reach. Who could tell? Perhaps they led to the Pole itself. There was little to lose, much to gain; he decided to risk it. Of course, it was not right, but we can easily understand it... the Belgica escaped undamaged...Modern scientific Antarctic exploration had now been initiated, and de Gerlache had won his place for all time in the first rank of Antarctic explorers."

5

THE NORTHWEST PASSAGE
PART ONE

Roald Amundsen kept working to get his captain's license so that he could lead an expedition. To qualify for this license, or "Master's Certificate," he had to spend more time at sea. He boarded one of his family's ships and sailed to Florida. Thinking about the future, Roald bought a supply of the best material for making sleds and skis: Florida hickory, a strong wood that bent like a bow.

Returning to Norway in 1900, Roald passed his Master's Certificate to become a captain.

He could now lead his own expedition.

The expedition he wanted was the one that his boyhood hero, John Franklin, had died attempting: sailing through the Northwest Passage.

By the end of the 1800s, it had not yet been done.

For this project Amundsen needed money, but people would not support his expedition unless he could make a contribution to science. As Amundsen wrote, "My expedition must have a scientific purpose as well as the purpose of exploration. Otherwise I should not be taken seriously and would not get backing."

The *Belgica* expedition had been interested in magnetism, and many discussions on board the ship had taught Amundsen about the topic. In 1831, forty years before Amundsen was born, an Englishman named James Ross found the North Magnetic Pole. Scientists wondered whether the Magnetic Poles moved, given that they were part of a force field. In order to answer this question, Amundsen decided to visit the North Magnetic Pole on his way through the Northwest Passage and compare the current position with that found 70 years before. Finding the North Magnetic Pole became the scientific reason why people gave money to Amundsen.

In 1900, Roald met with Fridtjof Nansen, the person who had first crossed that huge "glass mountain" called Greenland. By now, Nansen was the most famous living Norwegian explorer. Amundsen wrote, "Dr. Fridtjof Nansen, whose daring exploits… had made him the idol of my boyhood, was the Grand Old Man of Arctic exploration in Norway. I knew that a word of encouragement from him would be priceless to me in enlisting aid in my enterprise; on the other hand, a word of disparagement from him would be fatal."

Nansen gazed at Amundsen as he described his trip to the Antarctic and talked about his plans for the future. The two men discussed a Northwest Passage Expedition, and Nansen said he would write letters asking people to give money.

Roald needed training in how to use scientific instruments if he was to find the North Magnetic Pole, so he traveled to the German Marine Observatory in Hamburg to meet Professor Neumayer, one of the world's experts on magnetism. Amundsen explained to Professor Neumayer that he wanted to be the first person to sail through the Northwest Passage. The professor asked what else Amundsen wanted to do. Roald said he wanted to find the true location of the North Magnetic Pole. The professor then said "Young man, if you do that, you will be the benefactor of mankind." For three months, Professor Neumayer taught Amundsen the theory of magnetism and how to measure the location of the North Magnetic Pole.

Amundsen was almost ready to lead his expedition, but he needed a ship small enough to navigate the shallow waters and tight channels of the Arctic. In 1901, he used money left him by his father and mother to buy a wooden sailing vessel called *Gjoa*. The ship was twenty-nine years old, the same age as Amundsen, who took *Gjoa* on a sealing trip to earn money and learn how she sailed. Upon returning, he rebuilt the ship, adding an engine and a second, outside hull for protection from ice and rocks. This second hull would prove to be one of the smartest decisions Amundsen ever made.

The Gjoa

Fridtjof Nansen persuaded people to give money for the rebuilding of *Gjoa* and the purchase of German instruments for pinpointing the North Magnetic Pole. Nansen even asked the King of Sweden-Norway for help, which he gave.

Amundsen wanted expedition members experienced not just in sailing but in fixing an engine and taking magnetic measurements. Amundsen also wanted a good cook so everyone would enjoy their food and stay healthy.

He hired six expedition members:

Godfred Hansen, a naval officer and second in command to Amundsen. Hansen was said to laugh at everything, especially trouble.

The first mate, Anton Lund, was a navigator and expert on sailing in ice.

Amundsen had met the second mate and navigator after he walked past the "Admittance Forbidden" sign to look over the *Belgica* before it left for the Antarctic. Helmer Hanssen said, "Roald Amundsen was going to start for the Magnetic North Pole...before the New Year I heard I had the job...Amundsen came himself to the railway station in Christiana to meet me. His whole face was sunshine, and he gave me a hearty welcome. He was more like a kind father than a captain. He took me to the Sailors' Home and arranged for a room, and then we went on board *Gjoa* to meet the ship's company." Helmer Hanssen had splendid eyesight and could spot things long before others recognized them.

Peter Ristvedt had been Amundsen's sergeant during his military training and became the engineer in charge of the ship's motor.

The second engineer was Gustav Juel Wiik, a gunner in the Norwegian Navy who had also been trained at a magnetic observatory in Germany.

The cook was Adolf Henrik Lindstrom who had sailed on one Arctic expedition and was known for serving tender seal steaks and hot cakes from which the butter and red jam dripped.

Amundsen still needed more money. "I besieged every possible source of funds, the learned societies and private patrons of science. The rest of my time was spent in selecting and ordering supplies. Despair almost overcame me at times, because, in spite of everything, sufficient funds were not forthcoming. Some of the more impatient men from whom I had got supplies began pressing me for payment."

In June, 1903, the Norwegian economy was bad and companies were having trouble selling their products. Amundsen's biggest lender demanded his money back. Roald couldn't pay and didn't want his expedition to end before it began, but he was sure that he could earn enough money to pay people back after he returned to Norway. So, at midnight of the day the lender asked for his money, Roald, his six companions and his three brothers, who would sail up Christiana fjord as a way of saying goodbye, crept on board *Gjoa*, untied the lines, and slipped away. It was the first of Amundsen's deceptions.

He wrote "At last! The great adventure for which my whole life had been a preparation was underway!"

In the summer of 1903, the *Gjoa* reached Greenland and took on board a team of twenty huskies. Amundsen believed he could travel twice as fast as a man on foot by using dogs to pull light, strong sleds.

Amundsen stacked tanks of gasoline in the *Gjoa's* engine room. Boxes covered the deck. The ship floated so low that waves sloshed over the sides. *Gjoa* sailed into the Arctic Ocean.

Roald Amundsen's men liked him. Helmer Hanssen didn't know until later that Amundsen had had troubles with lenders back in Norway because Amundsen was so cheerful each day. Amundsen was the type of leader who did whatever his men did. Hanssen said "When dogs go loose on deck someone has to sweep up after them, but Amundsen never said to one of us: "Come and clean up after this dog." If he happened to be standing by he went and cleaned it up himself. If a rope fell off a pin he never gave an order to coil it up again. He did it himself."

Amundsen wrote, "We had no strict laws…Good work can be done without the fear of the law…I…let everyone feel that he was independent in his own sphere…the voyage of the "Gjoa" was far more like a holiday trip of comrades…" Yet, everyone knew that Amundsen was in charge. Helmer Hanssen wrote "In the daily life there were no distinctions of rank, and yet no one was ever in doubt about who was in command on board."

The expedition headed for Beechy Island and anchored at the last stopping place of John Franklin, Amundsen's childhood hero. This was the point from which the Englishman sailed into ice and to his death. On shore, crosses marked the graves of the men who had died from scurvy. Amundsen re-erected the only gravestone that had fallen down. He stayed up alone one night, sitting on the deck of Gjoa thinking about all that Franklin had done.

Franklin's Beechy Island Monument

The next day, Amundsen took measurements that placed the North Magnetic Pole in the direction of Boothia Peninsula. Amundsen decided that this would be the route he would take in trying to find the Northwest Passage.

The *Gjoa* set sail again, heading into the unknown waters of Peel Strait, which were free of ice but full of rocks. Along the coast of Boothia Peninsula engineer Peter Ristvedt reported that one of the gasoline tanks, stacked beside the engine, was leaking. Captain Amundsen took a look and asked Ristvedt to empty the leaking tank before the engine room filled with fumes and gasoline. Ristvedt did this, but left a pile of gas-soaked cleaning rags. Not much was known in those days about the dangers of spontaneous combustion. That evening, *Gjoa* anchored for the night near a small island. Amundsen was writing in his journal when he heard a shriek and ran up on deck. Flames roared and smoke billowed from the skylight covering the engine room. The men grabbed fire extinguishers and pumped with the strength of gorillas, pouring water onto the fire, thankful there was no leaking fuel to ignite but knowing the gas tanks were bombs waiting to explode. Down in the engine room, the pile of rags that had spontaneously burst into flames spluttered and hissed as the fire died away.

The smell of smoke lingered as *Gjoa* set sail next morning and headed into Wellington Strait between Boothia Peninsula and Matty Island. Amundsen was at the tiller, steering away from shallow water and small islands when *Gjoa* bumped rocks, scraped over them, and sailed free. Amundsen jerked the tiller, but the ship scraped again and shuddered to a stop. Amundsen rushed up the mast and climbed into the observation bucket called the "crow's nest." *Gjoa* had grounded on an underwater reef. Six feet of water covered the rocks but the ship, because of its heavy cargo, needed ten feet of water to float free. The edge of the reef was nine ship lengths ahead. Amundsen ordered the crew to throw cargo overboard, hoping that the wind would be strong enough to push a lighter *Gjoa* back into deep water.

Rocks gripped the ship.

Amundsen threw an anchor out from the side. It stuck fast on the reef. The crew pulled the anchor rope until *Gjoa* leaned over, but the ship remained stuck all that morning, through the afternoon, and throughout the night.

The following day, Amundsen came on deck to find a gale whipping white foam from the sea. The men jerked the anchor rope, but rocks still gripped the hull. The wind blew sheets of spray across the decks. Amundsen called his six comrades together for a talk. They decided to hoist all the sails and see if the wind would shove their ship across the reef, even though the push of canvas could break the mast.

The wind shrieked, waves pounded, and *Gjoa* lurched forward. It hit more rocks, and splinters of wood boiled up from underneath. Amundsen thought the hull would break.

Another wave lifted the boat and slammed it onto the reef.

The extra keel broke, and wood floated up.

Amundsen clung to the rail each time the ship pitched onto rocks. He was angry with himself. "If I had set a watch in the crow's nest, this would never have happened, because he would have observed the reef a long way off…"

Gjoa scraped and bumped over rocky teeth, bits of the hull breaking off and dancing in the waves. Ropes trembled, freezing rain turned the sails into lead weights, and the mast creaked.

Captain Amundsen now had to make a choice: either lower the lifeboats and escape, or risk the ship breaking up and the crew drowning. *Gjoa* crashed and bounced its way toward the end of the reef, but the rocks were now closer to the surface. Amundsen made his decision. He gave the order to lower the lifeboats and abandon ship.

On most vessels, the captain's order would have been law, and the crew would have got into the lifeboats. Yet Amundsen had told his men to always speak up. The first mate, Anton Lund, suggested they try once more to lighten the ship by throwing cargo overboard. Everyone agreed and heaved boxes into the water. Lieutenant Godfred Hansen gripped the tiller and spread his legs as a wave lifted *Gjoa* and flung her forward. The crew hung on. The ship bumped twice, a thump shook the timbers, and the hull slid off the rocks. Pieces of wood tumbled and frothed over the reef as *Gjoa* sailed away.

Amundsen scrambled up the mast to look for a path through the shallow waters. Hansen pulled on the tiller to turn the ship, but it drifted toward an island. Amundsen gazed at the back of *Gjoa*. The rudder had hit the end of the reef when the ship scraped over it. As *Gjoa* slid into deep water, rocks forced the rudder up until its pins popped out of the iron loops, called gudgeons, which held it to the hull. The rudder hadn't yet floated away because the pins now balanced on top of the gudgeons, just behind the loops, like a ballerina on the tips of her toes. Amundsen yelled at Hansen to hold the tiller straight so the rudder didn't fall off and leave *Gjoa* drifting toward the nearest rocks. Minutes went by as the men thought about what to do. *Gjoa* rose over a wave. The pins fell back into the gudgeons. The rudder had reattached itself. Godfred Hansen steered for deep water. When the men went below to check for leaks, they found a dry ship. What had saved the ship from breakup was Amundsen's decision to cover *Gjoa* with an extra hull.

Helmer Hanssen commented that throughout the grounding Amundsen had been a natural leader. "No praise could be too much for Amundsen's conduct during all these trials. It was his first expedition, but he was just a born natural leader."

On September 9, 1903, with a man in the crow's nest, *Gjoa* reached the entrance to Simpson Strait, which lay between King William Land and Adelaide Peninsula on the mainland of Canada. Amundsen turned his head. *Gjoa* had passed a small cove. Its narrow entrance would keep out heavy ice. Hills would block wind. It was the place to spend the winter and find the North Magnetic Pole before continuing through the Northwest Passage.

Gjoa glided into the cove. By early October, 1903, ice gripped the hull. Amundsen called the cove "Gjoahaven," meaning place of safety for the *Gjoa*.

Reaching Gjoahaven

6
THE NORTHWEST PASSAGE
PART TWO

Amundsen set his instruments up on shore and figured out that the North Magnetic Pole was 100 miles away. He decided to travel there once the seas had frozen, but first he had to learn to drive a team of dogs. Before doing that, he had to solve another problem: avoiding scurvy. Some of the expedition's provisions lay scattered around the reef. Amundsen wanted to find fresh meat, just like he had on board *Belgica*. The men went hunting caribou and were able to kill enough for a winter's supply of food.

By now snow had fallen, so Amundsen made his first dogsled trip, from the ship to the hunting grounds. He went back and forth, learning to drive a team of huskies. The men made a kennel for the dogs by digging out a snowdrift on shore and laying one of the lifeboats over top as a roof.

Amundsen and his men had brought woolen winter clothing and a supply of reindeer skin outer clothing. Since arriving at Gjoahaven, the men had been shooting reindeer for food, and had saved the calfskins, hoping to make soft underclothes. They attempted to spread the skins out to dry and then sew them, but didn't know the best way to go about it. A solution soon presented itself.

First Dogsled Trip

One morning, Amundsen came on deck and saw movement on the far hill. He squinted and decided it was a herd of reindeer. Godfred Hansen said the reindeer were walking on two legs. Five Inuit approached. Amundsen knew from books that an Inuit word "Teima" meant something like "good-day," but he wanted to be careful. He had read about explorers fighting with native people. Amundsen loaded his rifle and marched up the hill with Helmer Hanssen and Anton Lund. The Inuit were talking to each other, pointing, laughing, and making hand motions before spreading out in a line. Bows rested on their backs.

Amundsen called out, "Teima!"

The Inuit stopped.

Amundsen again called "Teima!"

The Inuit yelled, "Manik-tu-mi! Manik-tu-mi!"

Amundsen recognized the word as another friendly greeting. He flung his rifle down, a smile lifted his face, and he walked with arms open. Hanssen describes what happened next. "When we came right up to them they began to stroke our chests. They seemed to want to rub noses, but we did not dare to let them...The Inuit gesticulated and pointed towards the ship, and Amundsen then beckoned to them to follow us on board."

On the *Gjoa*, Chef Lindstrom offered coffee and biscuits. The Inuit used hand gestures to say that they wanted something else to drink. They swallowed water instead. Nor would they eat the biscuits after seeing the caribou piled on the deck. Amundsen offered a caribou leg. The Inuit drew long knives and feasted on the meat. They stayed overnight and left the following day.

That successful meeting was all Amundsen had hoped for. His willingness to learn from the natives was different from the attitude of British explorers at the time. The British believed in the power of their inventions to overcome all challenges, and would not accept that a native people might hold the key to Arctic exploration. This attitude would later contribute to the problems of Amundsen's great rival, a man named Scott.

It was now November. Amundsen was still experimenting with reindeer underclothing, and he decided to visit his Inuit friends to find out more about how they lived. He went alone and without weapons to show that he trusted them, a brave thing to do for someone who had not spent much time with native people. The Inuit lived in a valley, where they had built six igloos beside an ice-covered lake. They shrieked and rushed to meet Amundsen as he walked toward them. When the natives reached the tall Norwegian, they stared into his face, grabbed at his clothes, and stroked him. The men led the Norwegian into an igloo, where Amundsen joined them in feasting on raw caribou. After the men had eaten, women came in and greeted Amundsen with the word "Manik-tu-mi." They smiled and touched the tall Viking.

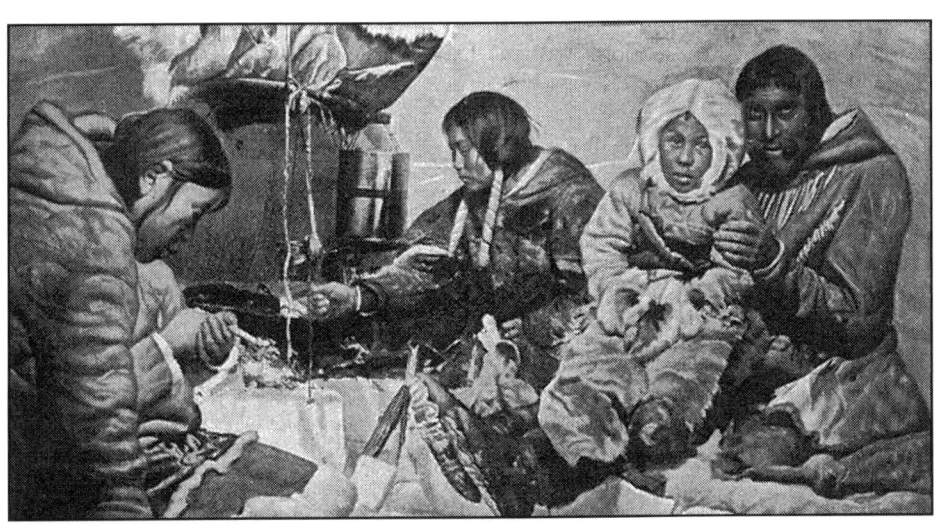

Eskimo Family in Igloo

Amundsen stayed one day before returning to Gjoahaven. He slept in an igloo and found out how warm it was. After this, the Inuit visited the Norwegians many times. Amundsen learned more and more about the things Astrup had lectured on at Christiana University ten years before: Inuit clothing, igloos, dogsleds, and skis.

Amundsen bought a complete set of Inuit fur clothing. He wanted to see if it was as warm as Dr. Cook had said. It was. Compared to woolen Norwegian clothing, the skins dried more easily, needed less washing, kept wind out, and felt warm the moment you put them on. Amundsen concluded that "the Eskimo (Inuit) dress in winter in these regions is far superior to our European clothes. But one must either wear it all or not at all....Woollen underclothing absorbs all the perspiration and soon becomes wet...Dressed in nothing but reindeer skin, like the Eskimo, and with garments so loose and roomy on the body that air can circulate between them, one can generally keep things dry."

Amundsen learned to wear an animal skin coat with the fur turned inside so it didn't trap snow that would otherwise melt and wet the clothing.

He wore caribou fur underwear.

Amundsen, Hansen, and Ristvedt at Gjoahaven

Amundsen now knew which clothes he was going to wear on the sledding trip to the North Magnetic Pole, but he worried that his tents wouldn't keep out the deep cold of the Arctic winter. He wanted to learn how to build an igloo.

On Christmas Day, the Inuit band moved from their valley. An old man, Teraiu, came to the ship, tears running down his cheeks. He had been among the group of five that first met Amundsen. The band had left him behind. Rather than let Teraiu starve, Amundsen gave him food and asked for igloo-building lessons. Each morning Amundsen, Hanssen, and Ristvedt carved snow. The Inuit taught the Norwegians to build an igloo in ninety minutes. Amundsen used a long knife to cut snow blocks two feet long, about a foot high, and four inches thick. Stacking the blocks in a circle, Amundsen built each layer leaning inwards to create a shape like a beehive, moving higher and higher until a hole remained in the top. Amundsen then took a block of snow into the igloo, jiggled it up through the hole, held it with one hand, carved it, and let it fall into place. Finally, Amundsen lit a lamp inside the igloo to melt the snow between the blocks and let them freeze tight

Meanwhile, Chef Lindstrom was busy cooking platters of fresh meat, mounds of his famous hotcakes, and jugs of hot coffee. There were no signs of scurvy.

Unfortunately, the dogs did not do as well as the men. Seven huskies died by Christmas. Amundsen didn't know what caused the deaths but thought perhaps the dogs hadn't eaten enough fatty meat. On March 1, 1904, with the temperature at 63 below zero Fahrenheit, Amundsen, Helmer Hanssen, Godfred Hansen, and Peter Ristvedt loaded their sleds, which were made of the hickory wood that Amundsen had bought in Florida, and set out to find the North Magnetic Pole. There were only enough dogs to pull one sled. Helmer Hanssen guided the huskies, while Hansen, Ristvedt and Amundsen man-hauled the second sled. Amundsen had hoped to avoid this type of pulling after his experience on Brabant Island during the *Belgica* expedition. He crept along like a snail. Soft snow gripped the sleds like paste, and the men had to jerk them free.

Gjoa Expedition Native Clothing

Meanwhile, Helmer Hanssen showed that he knew how to drive a dog team. Whenever the huskies tired, Hanssen walked to the front of the sled and pulled alongside until the animals hauled again. By mid-afternoon the men had pulled enough, and the very cold air had tired the dogs.

Amundsen built an igloo to stay warm. Around the snow hut was "stillness, with the western sky in a dying glow of green and the stars growing in brightness." The men knocked the snow off their clothes and crept into their igloo to cook their food, separated by an ice wall from the frost outside.

That night the temperature dropped to minus 79 Fahrenheit, far below the minus 10 that Roald and Leon had faced their first night on Hardangervidda when prying open the nailed door of the midway hut. It was so cold that the dogs found it difficult to uncurl from their sleeping spots in the snow. In the morning, when Amundsen removed a glove, his fingers turned white quicker than a lobster turns red in a pot of boiling water. The men set out again, pulling into the wind and checking their noses for frostbite. After a few miles, they stopped and built another igloo. On the third morning, the temperature was still too low. Amundsen was not going to make the mistake he had made on Hardangervidda by continuing when it was too dangerous. He put some food and one of the two sleds inside the igloo, walled it up to protect the supplies for another trip, and turned around. With the dogs pulling only one sled, the men took four hours instead of two and a half days to return the seven miles to Gjoahaven.

Port Gjoa

Amundsen decided that he would never man-haul a sled again. From now on, he took only one person with him on a trip so that food and equipment were light enough for his few remaining dogs to pull.

In April, 1904, Amundsen and Peter Ristvedt set out to find the Magnetic Pole. Teraiu went along the first day, walking in front of the dogs, which pulled hard after the Inuit. The second day, Teraiu left to find his tribe in their summer hunting grounds, and the huskies no longer wanted to pull as hard. Amundsen remembered what Teraiu had done, so the Norwegian walked in front of the dog team. The huskies pulled hard once again. The two men traveled across the frozen Wellington Strait to Matty Island, near where *Gjoa* had hit the reef. They set up their instruments and took magnetic measurements. Then they traveled up the coast of Boothia past the spot where James Ross located the old Magnetic Pole, and found that it was no longer there.

It had shifted north.

Amundsen had proved that Magnetic Poles move.

Off Matty Island, Amundsen and Ristvedt met Inuit who had caught some seals. They gave fresh meat and blubber to the dogs, who gorged themselves and then pulled the sled like it carried no load.

Amundsen traveled north and took more measurements near the Tasmania Islands. He moved around the area for three weeks trying to locate the North Magnetic Pole, but could not do so.

As summer approached, Amundsen and Gustav Wiik took magnetic measurements near the ship and at other places to get data for Professor Neumayer.

Amundsen was also waiting for the ice to go out so *Gjoa* could finish sailing through the Northwest Passage.

The summer was a cold one, with very little open water for navigation. In August ice still blocked Gjoahaven, so Helmer Hanssen and Godfred Hansen set off in a lifeboat to find a route for *Gjoa*. They returned in early September, having discovered a way through the Simpson Strait. But the ice around Gjoahaven thickened. By September 21, the second winter had begun.

Amundsen learned everything he could about living in the Arctic. Eighteen Inuit families built igloos near the ship, so it was easy to study their ways. The Norwegians experimented with various dog foods and confirmed that huskies were healthiest when eating fatty, fresh meat. Helmer Hanssen and the others became good dog sledders. Amundsen learned how the Inuit made their sleds glide in sticky snow by coating the runners with a mixture of moss and water, then wetting a bearskin mitten with mouth-warmed water to build up more layers of ice. The Norwegians practiced skiing. They built better igloos in less time. The Inuit taught them how to fish from the ice and creep up on deer. They showed the Norwegians their tools. These skills would later prove invaluable to Amundsen when he explored a different part of the world.

Early in 1905, Amundsen found a fault in a magnetic instrument, which he tried to correct. He took more measurements for Professor Neumayer. Amundsen, because of the flawed instrumentation, had missed finding the new location of the North Magnetic Pole by thirty miles.

The summer of 1905 was warmer than 1904, and on August 13 the ice went out. Hanssen describes the departure: "All the Eskimos gathered on the beach, and ran alongside us as we got under way. Those who had kayaks jumped into them, and accompanied us across the harbor. As long as we could hear and see them, they called out greetings of farewell."

Gjoa sailed into Simpson Strait, following Godfred Hansen and Helmer Hanssen's route from the summer before. Amundsen wrote, "We jumped, so to speak, right into the same doubtful navigation as before, impenetrable fog, no compass, and a very changeable breeze, which was therefore a poor guide…I put Hanssen and Lund on the look-out in the crow's nest, they being the best qualified men for the job." Amundsen and Godfred Hansen took turns steering *Gjoa* between King William Land and the Adelaide Peninsula. Amundsen commented again: "I believe this was our most exciting passage. It was getting shallower and shallower up towards the Sound, but our look-out man reported deeper water beyond the reef we had to pass. The helm went from board to board the whole time, just as if we were in thick ice…During the lovely afternoon we had more breathing space again; it had become broiling hot and the sea was perfectly calm. Small lumps of ice were pitching and nodding here and there on the water, with a blue-green reflection in the sun…During the evening some ice made its appearance from the south, and presently the whole sea to the south was covered."

Amundsen followed the edge of the pack ice into Queen Maud's Sea toward the Nordenskjold Islands. He had hoped to sail to the south of these islands, but the ice forced him up and around to the north. Fortunately the water was deep. On the morning of August 15, ice forced *Gjoa* to sail straight into a group of islands rather than going around them. "We were in the midst of a most disconcerting chaos; sharp stones face us on every side, low-lying rocks of all shapes, and we bungled through zig-zag as if drunk… the man at the helm had to pay very close attention and keep his eye on the look-out man who jumped about in the crow's nest like a maniac, throwing his arms to starboard and port respectively.…

Now I see a big shallow extending from one islet right over to the other. We must get up to it and see. The anchors were clear to drop, should the water be too shallow, and we proceeded at a very slow rate. I was at the helm and kept shuffling my feet out of sheer nervousness. We barely managed to scrape over."

That evening, *Gjoa* reached Victoria Strait, leaving the islands behind. The Strait was full of ice floes, but loose enough for the ship to push through. *Gjoa* anchored on August 17 by Cape Colborne, the furthest point reached by a ship coming into the Northwest Passage from the other way: the direction of Alaska. Again Amundsen wrote, "this was a significant day in the history of our Expedition – for we had now sailed the "Gjoa" *through the hitherto unsolved link in the North West Passage*. We now felt we had got back again to fairly-known waters, so to speak. A sounding was now and then given on the chart…"

Still, the Gjoa had tricky navigation ahead, with shallow waters and ragged stone bottoms. It was not until a few days later that Amundsen could report, "My relief at having thus got clear of the last difficult hole in the North West Passage was indescribable. I cannot deny that I had felt very nervous during the last few days. The thought that here in these troublesome waters we were running the risk of spoiling the whole of our so far successful enterprise was anything but pleasant."

At 8 in the morning of August 27, Amundsen finished his watch and went below to sleep. "I became conscious of a rushing to and fro on the deck…Lieutenant Hansen came rushing down into the cabin and called out the memorable words: "Vessel in sight, sir!" He bolted again immediately, and I was alone. The North West Passage had been accomplished – my dream from childhood. This very moment it was fulfilled. I had a peculiar sensation in my throat; I was somewhat overworked and tired, and I suppose it was weakness on my part, but I could feel tears coming to my eyes."

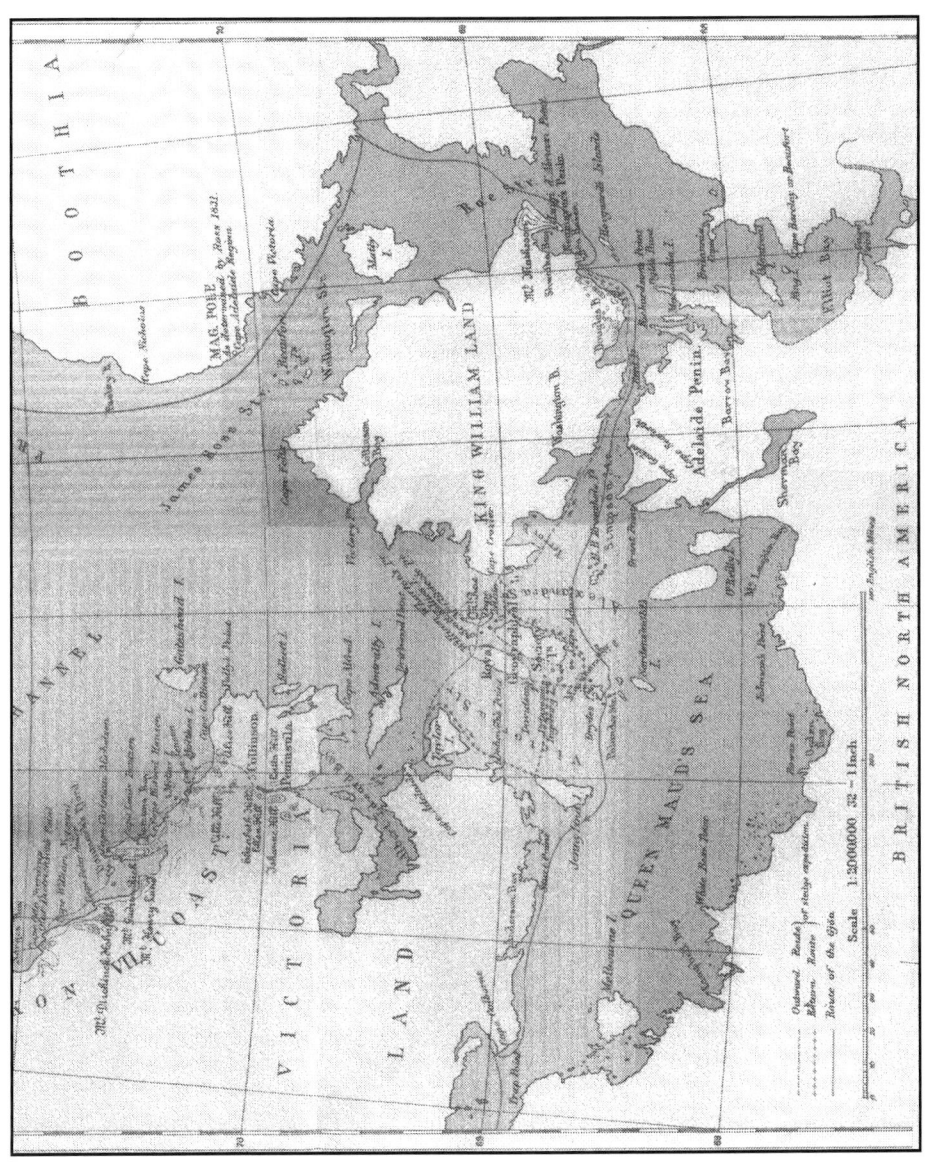

Amundsen jumped into his clothes and rushed up to the deck. The vessels were rapidly approaching each other. The Stars and Stripes flapped on the *Charles Hanson* of San Francisco. "An elderly man with a white beard advanced towards me on the quarter deck. He was newly shaven, and nicely dressed, evidently the master of the ship. "Are you Captain Amundsen?" was his first remark. I was quite surprised to hear that we were known so far away and answered in the affirmative, owning that I was the man. "Is this the first vessel you have met?" the old man asked. And when I admitted it was so, his countenance brightened up. We shook hands long and heartily. "I am exceedingly pleased to be the first one to welcome you on getting through the North West Passage.""

The Gjoa's first meeting with Whalers after completing the North West Passage

7
PLANNING
FOR THE NORTH POLE

The *New York Times* wrote on December 10, 1905, that Captain Amundsen had "the boldness to conceive, the courage to attempt, and the good luck to achieve the first voyage by a single vessel through the Northwest Passage... Those will best appreciate his success who have read of the prodigious effort and the enormous treasure that were expended for three centuries to find the Northwest Passage."

In October, 1906, Amundsen and his men arrived in Christiana as heroes. They stepped from the ironclad Norwegian warship *Norge* onto a red carpet and walked to carriages that rolled them past cheering crowds. Christiana's fortress fired a fifteen gun salute. A banquet was given in Amundsen's honor.

During the year that followed, Amundsen gave lectures in the United States and Europe, earning enough money to pay back all he owed, including to the man who had nearly prevented *Gjoa* from leaving Norway on that night in June, 1903. In November, 1906, the Norwegian Society of New York gave Amundsen a banquet. Norwegian and American flags decorated the tables. President Roosevelt sent a letter to the society president, which he read. "May I thru you and thru the Norwegian Society of New York greet your guest, Capt. Roald Amundsen, and congratulate him on the notable feat he has accomplished. With all good wishes to him and also to your society, believe me, sincerely yours, Theodore Roosevelt."

Having paid his debts, Amundsen was free to plan his next expedition. He wrote, "The next exploit which I resolved to attempt was the capture of the North Pole."

Fridtjof Nansen had, after crossing Greenland, led an expedition that tried to reach the North Pole, a part of the world covered by the Arctic Ocean, which is in turn covered with ice. Nansen built a ship with rounded sides so that sea ice would lift rather than squeeze the hull. He and his crew sailed the ship, called the *Fram*, into the Arctic ice and drifted with ocean currents. When he thought he was close to the Pole, Nansen climbed out of his ship and traveled by dogsled and kayak, but had to turn back about three hundred miles from his goal.

Robert Edwin Peary, the American explorer, had also failed to reach the North Pole. He used dog sleds to travel from northern Canada over the frozen Arctic Ocean.

Amundsen considered both methods. He decided to try Nansen's way, but enter the sea ice at a different place, Alaska, in hopes of drifting closer to the North Pole. He asked Nansen if he could use the *Fram* because of its special hull design. By now Sweden no longer ruled Norway, and Nansen was living in London as the Norwegian Ambassador to England. He couldn't leave his job for another try at reaching the North Pole, so he asked the Norwegian government, which owned the *Fram*, to let Amundsen use the ship.

Amundsen planned to leave Norway in 1910 and sail south through the Atlantic Ocean. The Panama Canal was still being built, so the *Fram* would go around Cape Horn before heading north again to San Francisco and entering the Arctic ice from Alaska. Amundsen was ready to spend up to five years drifting over the top of the world and making a scientific survey of the Arctic Ocean on the way to the North Pole. The explorer took an oceanography course to prepare himself in a similar way to when he learned about magnetism. He found out how to measure an ocean's width and depth, examine what the water is made of and how it moves, and study the creatures that live in it.

Although Roald Amundsen never married, he did fall in love at this time with a woman called Sigrid Castberg, who lived in Christiana. She was married. Roald wanted her to divorce her husband and marry him. She decided not to.

Roald Amundsen

The Norwegian government made its decision about the *Fram*. It gave the ship and some money to Amundsen. Other people made contributions, and Amundsen borrowed, but he still didn't have enough funds to reach the North Pole. Nevertheless, the famous explorer began refitting the *Fram* and asking people to join him on his expedition.

On his way to give a lecture in 1909, Amundsen changed trains in Germany and found the Norwegian National Ski Team in the station. One of its members was Olav Bjaaland who, at Norway's famous Holmenkollen Ski Festival, had skied ten miles and jumped more than sixty feet to win the gold medal in the Nordic Combined Event. Amundsen asked Bjaaland to join his expedition. Bjaaland agreed. In addition to his skiing skills, the champion was also a carpenter who made skis and violins.

It was then that the American explorer Peary announced that he had reached the North Pole.

Amundsen's reaction was as follows:

"It was in September, 1909, that the news reached us. At the same instant I saw quite clearly that the original plan of the *Fram's* third voyage – the exploration of the North Polar basin – hung in the balance. If the expedition was to be saved, it was necessary to act quickly and without hesitation. Just as rapidly as the message had travelled over the cables I decided on my change of front – to turn to the right-about, and face to the South.

It was true that I had announced in my plan that the *Fram's* third voyage would be in every way a scientific expedition, and would have nothing to do with record-breaking; it was also true that many of the contributors who had so warmly supported me had done so with the original plan before them; but in view of the altered circumstances, and the small prospect I now had of obtaining funds for my original plan, I considered it neither mean nor unfair to my supporters to strike a blow that would at once put the whole enterprise on its feet, retrieve the heavy expenses that the expedition had already incurred, and save the contributions from being wasted.

It was therefore with a clear conscience that I decided to postpone my original plan for a year or two, in order to try in the meantime to raise the funds that were still lacking. The North Pole, the last problem but one of popular interest in Polar exploration, was solved. If I was now to succeed in arousing interest in my undertaking, there was nothing left for me but to try to solve the last great problem – the South Pole."

The race was on, although the British didn't yet know that it involved Amundsen.

The New York Times reported (September 13, 1909) that "Britain Wants South Pole," and quoted the British explorer Captain Robert Scott as saying "Through the energy and daring of Commander Peary the hope that the Union Jack would fly first at the north pole has been taken from us forever…The people of this country are unaccustomed to take second place in any field of human endeavor, but if Peary's great exploit is to be rivaled the south pole alone remains as our sphere of action. A race for it is certain in the immediate future."

The same month that Peary reached the North Pole, Captain Scott announced that he would lead his second British Expedition to the world's most southern continent. Scott's objective, as stated in the expedition prospectus, was "to reach the South Pole and to secure for the British Empire the honour of this achievement."

Further objectives were scientific research and geographical exploration. *The New York Times* reported (September 13, 1909) that the British explorer would take ponies, dogs, and motor sleds, "It is stated that if motor sledges can reach the foot of a glacier there can be little doubt they will ascend it and greatly simplify the journey."

Amundsen kept his game plan a secret. It was his second deception. Amundsen had good reasons, just like he had for starting the Northwest Passage expedition in spite of his lender's demands.

Norway was a new and small country that depended on Britain's friendship to protect it from invasion. Britain ruled an empire, and some British believed that the part of Antarctica discovered by Sir James Ross, the same person who had found the North Magnetic Pole in 1831, should not be used by other countries. The first person to land in this area had actually been the Norwegian captain of a British expedition. In 1900, Carstens Borchgrevink had climbed onto the Ross Ice Shelf at a place called The Bay of Whales and used dogsleds to explore towards the South Pole.

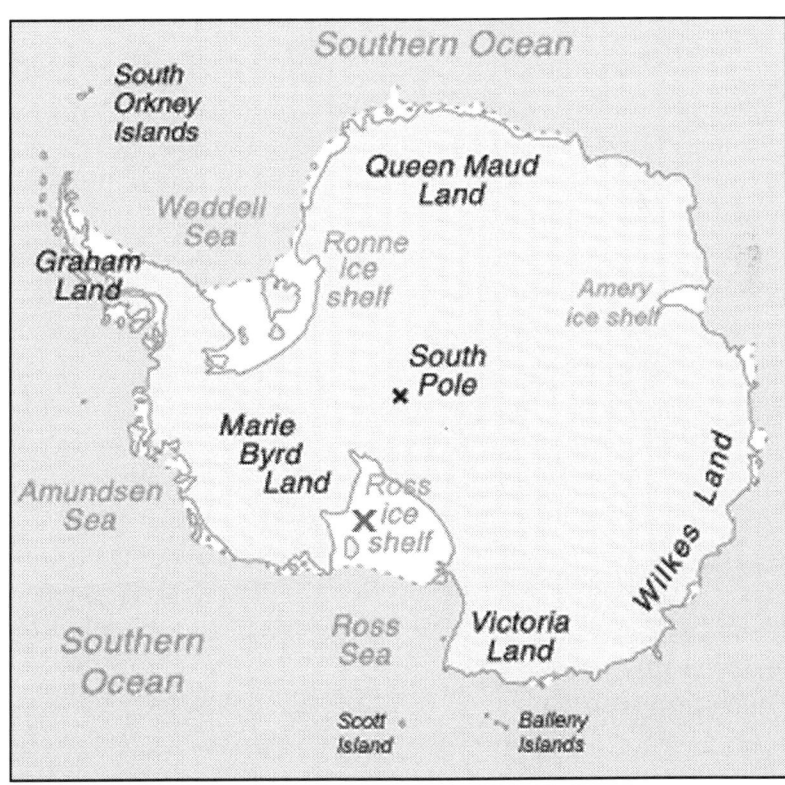

Amundsen wanted to start his journey from the Ross Sea because it was the closest point to the South Pole that a ship could reach. Yet he didn't want to retrace the steps of British expeditions. Even though he would blaze his own trail in Antarctica, Amundsen worried that if the Norwegian government heard about his change of plans, they might take both the *Fram* and his money away rather than anger the British government. Also, Captain Amundsen probably wanted to keep his plans secret from Captain Scott. It was after all, as Scott had stated it, a race. Nevertheless, the Norwegian's lack of scientific purpose that was such an important part of exploration in those days, combined with Amundsen's secrecy, would make the British criticize the Viking explorer.

Amundsen continued to talk with men whom he wanted to join his expedition. He visited the best dogsledder he knew: his companion through the Northwest Passage, Helmer Hanssen. Hanssen agreed to join the expedition, and, having his mate's certificate, signed on as *Fram's* ice pilot. Amundsen wrote to Adolf Lindstrom, *Gjoa's* chef, who returned from a fishing trip in Alaska to join up. Oscar Wisting, a naval gunner who had helped re-fit *Fram*, also joined the expedition. He had his mate's certificate, could re-build almost anything, and could ski and sled.

Amundsen worked out all the details of the trip. He didn't believe he could reach the South Pole and return safely without huskies. Ever since Astrup's lecture at Christiana University many years before, Amundsen had learned again and again that dogs, not men, should pull sleds. He had man-hauled a sled on the *Belgica* expedition and done it early that first winter at Gjoahaven. Amundsen knew that a dog team with men on skis could travel twice as fast as men on foot pulling a sled. There was, however, one problem that Amundsen and his men would talk a lot about: should they kill many of their huskies during the South Pole journey to provide fresh meat to the remaining dogs? Other explorers had written about the need to do this.

Peary had used huskies to pull his sleds both in Greenland and across the sea ice to the North Pole. The American explorer had killed some of his huskies to feed the other dogs.

In 1901, Captain Scott led the first British Antarctic Expedition and took with him nineteen dogs to pull the sleds. He set off on a trip partway to the South Pole and killed his dogs one by one to feed the others. He commented, "There is no real reason why the life of a dog should be considered more than that of a sheep, and no one would pause to consider the cruelty of driving a diminishing flock of sheep to supply the wants and aid the movement of travelers."

Amundsen knew from his trips out of Gjoahaven that huskies needed fresh meat to stay strong. Rather than killing seals and pulling them on sleds to the South Pole, a weight that would make the journey last longer and risk human lives, Amundsen made his choice. He wrote, "fifty pounds of edible food in the carcass of an Eskimo dog…meant fifty less pounds of food to be carried." He decided that he would kill most of his dogs during the journey to the South Pole in order to feed the remaining dogs. Amundsen also decided to unload some of the food from the sleds and store it in depots all along the route. Other explorers had written and lectured about the need to do this. Fewer huskies would be needed to pull the lightened sleds on the trip back from the Pole because the expedition members would get their food from the depots.

Amundsen thought about which breed of husky he should use.

Around Gjoahaven, when Amundsen man-hauled the sled, the temperatures had been close to minus seventy degrees Fahrenheit. It had been too cold for the dogs. Amundsen now chose North Greenland huskies because they could work in the lowest temperatures: fifty degrees below zero. Amundsen would turn back or rest if it got colder than that.

In July, 1910, ninety-nine huskies arrived in Norway. Amundsen thought the most handsome of all was Colonel, a strong, reddish brown husky. Chef Lindstrom took care of the dogs on a small island until *Fram* was ready to sail. The government also sent one of its employees, Sverre Hassel, to help care for the huskies and make sure Amundsen didn't break the law by letting the dogs leave the island before going on board *Fram*.

Hassel was an expert dogsled driver who had been on expeditions before getting his government job. Amundsen wanted him to drive one of the sleds to the South Pole, and persuaded the government to promise Hassel that he could have his job back if he joined the *Fram* expedition. Hassel agreed to go along and take care of the dogs, but only as far as San Francisco. He did not know that Amundsen had decided to go to the South Pole.

Sverre Hassel

Amundsen kept on organizing his expedition. He made his own food: pemmican with dried meat, fat, vegetables, and oatmeal. He made dog food with fish or meat, fat, and dried milk. He ordered ten sleds to be made in Christiana. He bought Greenland sealskin clothing and twenty pairs of skis. Knowing how difficult it was to put a tent up in a snowstorm, Amundsen ordered a design that only had one pole. 250 reindeer skins went into fur clothing and sleeping bags. Large boots allowed two pairs of socks to be worn inside them. Amundsen built a house to serve as winter Antarctic quarters, took it apart, and stored the pieces on board the *Fram*.

Amundsen still didn't have enough money for his expedition, so it was a wonderful surprise when a rich Norwegian who wanted to help explorers, Don Pedro Christopherson, gave the money and supplies necessary. Amundsen didn't tell Christopherson of the expedition's change of plans, but when Don Pedro later heard that the South Pole had become the objective, his support was enthusiastic.

By August, 1910, *Fram* was ready. The dogs gave howling concerts on their island, and visitors came to see them, feeding sandwiches to the huskies. Oscar Wisting took over from Sverre Hassel in helping Chef Lindstrom take care of the dogs. One day, Colonel leaped into the sea and swam toward the mainland, heading for a flock of sheep and a good meal of fresh meat. Wisting and Lindstrom jumped into a boat and rowed after Colonel. The dog had powered halfway to the sheep when the men caught up, leaned over, grabbed him, and tussled him into the boat. Wisting liked Colonel so much that on another day he went swimming with him.

On August 9, 1910, Wisting and Lindstrom took twenty dogs at a time by boat from the island to *Fram*. People who had visited the huskies worried that big waves would wash them off the ship during the voyage. Amundsen ordered that the dogs be chained to the deck in groups of ten. He brought a large canvas cover for shade once *Fram* reached the hotter parts of the world. One or two men took care of each group of dogs. Amundsen put himself in charge of fourteen huskies. Wisting made sure that Colonel was among the huskies he cared for.

As *Fram* set sail on its five month voyage to the bottom of the world, Amundsen told his men to remember that whenever they were deciding what to do, they had to start by taking care of the huskies. It was "Dogs first, and dogs all the time."

Dogs on Board Fram

The crew washed the decks twice a day. Colonel and the other huskies got used to the ship. Colonel howled each morning when Wisting came to him, and barked at the rattle of food dishes. When one husky howled, the others joined in a concert that woke the soundest sleeper. After several minutes, the dogs stopped their chorus as if an order had been given. Three weeks into the voyage, the first puppies were born. One after another, men came up on deck after dinner and fed scraps of their meal to the blue-eyed bundles of fur.

Dogs on Board

As the *Fram* neared the Portuguese island of Madeira, Amundsen worried that Sverre Hassel would leave the expedition when he heard that *Fram* was not going directly to San Francisco. Amundsen had told only a few people about his real plans and decided to pledge Hassel to secrecy, then tell him the truth. Amundsen told Hassel that he could leave the *Fram* at Madeira if he wanted to go home. A smile crinkled Hassel's cheeks. He stayed with the expedition.

Amundsen got ready to tell everyone else about the change of plans. The success of his expedition to the South Pole now depended on how well he explained his reasons for lying about going to the North Pole.

Fram sailed into Madeira's port and dropped anchor.

8
Heading
to the South Pole

One of Amundsen's biographers, Bellamy Partridge, said about Roald Amundsen: "The men who went on journeys of exploration were loyal to him. They appreciated him and understood him. And he loved and trusted them."

Propeller repairs kept *Fram* in Madeira for a few days. On the morning the work was finished, Amundsen told his crew they would be leaving that same evening. The men began writing their letters home. Three hours ahead of departure, the windlass began pulling on the anchor chain. Everyone dropped their pens and rushed on deck, thinking that they had misheard the time the ship would be leaving port. Captain Amundsen stood in front of a map of Antarctica ready to make the most difficult speech of his life. The pale blue eyes of the eagle-nosed Viking drifted over the crowd. As Hanssen tells it, "He said he had deceived us and also the Norwegian nation. But that could not be helped…Anyone on board who didn't want to go to the South Pole was at liberty to leave the ship right away and go back to Norway…"

Amundsen explained that since the North Pole had been reached, they would race the British to the South Pole. Someone yelled "Hurrah!" Amundsen's blue eyes rested on Olav Bjaaland. The Norwegian ski champion loved a race. "That means we'll get there first!"

Amundsen asked each man if he would make the detour to the South Pole. Each one said yes. Amundsen's heart must have pounded with relief. He then gave everyone an hour to finish their letters. He notified Fridtjof Nansen and also King Haakon VII of Norway that the expedition intended to plant the Norwegian flag at the South Pole. Amundsen explained that he would not follow the same route as earlier British expeditions, but would try a new way. The Norwegian explorer also sent a message to Captain Scott, who by now had reached Australia on his way to Antarctica.

Fram upped anchor and set sail. A cooling wind welcomed the ship and pulled a howling concert from Colonel and the other huskies.

On The Way To The Pole

Amundsen believed that explorers should become "informed regarding the experience of all preceding expeditions. This knowledge in my own case has several times saved me from serious mistakes." He asked every man on board to read about previous expeditions. Books on Antarctica filled the ship's library, especially ones about Captain Scott and another British explorer called Ernest Shackleton. In 1908/09, Shackleton had crossed the ice shelf that covered the Ross Sea, climbed through the coastal mountains, traveled over the coldest place in the world, the Antarctic Plateau, but turned back one hundred and twelve miles from the South Pole due to lack of food.

As Amundsen's men read the books, they learned more about the Ross Ice Shelf, or Great Ice Barrier. The Ice Barrier was larger than the state of California, covering the sea for hundreds of miles out from land and ending with ice cliffs that towered more than twice the height of *Fram's* tallest mast. The edge of the Ice Barrier was the closest place to the South Pole that a ship could reach. Both Scott and Shackleton described a snow surface that convinced Olav Bjaaland it would be perfect for skiing.

Scott's British expedition also intended to cross the Barrier on the journey to the South Pole. Scott worried about making his base camp on a piece of ice that could calve, or break off from the shelf and drift out to sea, so he decided to set up camp on land at the edge of the Barrier in a place called McMurdo Sound.

Amundsen had another idea. He wrote, "I had been greatly struck with the discovery that the Bay of Whales, notwithstanding that it was merely a bay whose shores were the icy walls of the glacier, had not substantially changed its shore line since its first discovery by Sir James Ross in 1842...the glacier at this point must be firmly wedged upon the solid rock of some great and immovable island." Amundsen was going to try to set up his base camp on the Barrier, where the Norwegian explorer Borchgrevink had climbed up, so that he could start his journey sixty miles closer to the South Pole than the British at McMurdo Sound. Amundsen believed he had found a place where the ice pushed down through the Ross Sea and grounded itself on the bottom or perhaps on a small island. The Bay of Whales hadn't changed in seventy-eight years. Surely the ice cliffs would stay together and not send Amundsen and his winter hut drifting out to sea?

Fram headed south into warm weather. The men put the canvas awning up to protect the dogs from the sun's heat. Deck chains had held Colonel and the other huskies for six weeks, taming them, or so the men thought. Amundsen decided it was time to put muzzles over the dogs' mouths and let them loose to get more exercise. Those muzzles proved to be a smart idea. By this time, the dogs were used to their packs of ten, each of which had a leader. By unchaining them, the men were allowing any dog to move around the deck and thereby threaten the territory of another pack. Amundsen described what took place:

"At first nothing at all happened; it looked as if they had abandoned once for all the thought of ever moving from the spot they had occupied so long. At last a solitary individual had the bright idea of attempting a walk along the deck. But he should not have done so; it was dangerous to move about here. The unaccustomed sight of a loose dog at once aroused his nearest neighbours. A dozen of them flung themselves upon the unfortunate animal who had been the first to leave his place, rejoicing in the thought of planting their teeth in his sinful body. But to their disappointment the enjoyment was not so great as they expected. The confounded strap round their jaws made it impossible to get hold of the skin; the utmost they could do was to pull a few tufts of hair out of the object of their violent onslaught."

The battle lasted two hours without harming any dog. After fighting, the huskies moved about, stretching their legs, before hiding in every hole and corner on the *Fram*. There was hardly fur to be seen. Dogs made twenty-five foot leaps, the height of a house, down into the ship. One husky leaped below the deck and curled up between the piston rods of the engine. Fortunately, the engine was not started before the men found that dog.

Amundsen continued, "Before we let the dogs loose we had remarked that there were a few who, for some reason or other, did not seem as happy as they should have been: they were more shy and restless than the others…The day we let them loose we discovered what had been the matter…they had some old friend who had chanced to be placed in some other part of the deck…It was really touching to see the joy they showed on meeting again; they became quite different animals."

It got colder as *Fram* approached Antarctica. In rain storms, Colonel would stand for hours beside the main mast, with two of his dog friends, Suggen and Arne, rather than curl up on a wet deck. He and his pals would sleep day and night when the sun came out.

On January 11, 1911, during the Antarctic summer, the lookout in the crow's nest spotted the Ice Barrier, shining like a crystal Great Wall of China. *Fram* chugged along the Barrier and on

January 15 motored into a wide bay surrounded by walls of ice. Whales hissed and spouted. Seals lay on foot ice that had frozen over the surface of the sea for a mile and a half beyond the white cliffs. *Fram* came to a stop at the edge of the foot ice. Amundsen had reached the Bay of Whales. In the Arctic, Amundsen had called his camp Gjoahaven, or place of safety for *Gjoa*. In the Antarctic, Amundsen called his icy base Framheim, or home of the *Fram*.

Fram at the Ice Barrier

9
Preparing to Leave for the Pole

In the Bay of Whales, Amundsen left the *Fram* and skied over the foot ice, expecting to reach an ice wall two hundred feet high. Instead, he skied up a hill of snow that had drifted in and filled the space between the foot ice and the Barrier. A flock of Adelie penguins shot out of the water and slid across the ice to watch the Norwegian explorer find a place for the expedition's winter house.

Framheim

Dogs pulled supplies from the *Fram* to the base camp. Seals provided fresh meat for men and huskies. The sled track to the camp looked like a Norwegian country road.

Barrier Camp

On February 4, Scott's ship sailed into Bay of Whales. It was on an exploration voyage after dropping Scott and his supplies off at McMurdo Bay ten days before the Norwegians arrived at the Barrier. Scott was on land making plans that were very different from Amundsen's.

Robert Scott, being British, had grown up in a country with a milder climate than Norway's. Scott had seen little snow. He was over thirty when he skied for the first time. Like Amundsen, Scott was a captain and an experienced explorer who had spent two years in the Antarctic after Amundsen returned from the *Belgica* expedition. Scott had traveled partway over the Ice Barrier, suffered from scurvy, tried dog sledding, and dealt with deep cold. On this, his second expedition, he intended to reach the South Pole by following Shackleton's route and then continuing on for the final ninety-seven miles.

Scott, like other British explorers, believed there was no need to learn from native peoples because British inventions could solve any problem. Scott trusted machinery and knew a lot about it. During his training in the British navy, Scott learned about engines and commanded a torpedo boat before moving up to bigger ships. Unfortunately, Scott was not a competent captain, having run one of his ships aground, endangered another in Antarctica, and collided a third. He paid little attention to details, and was too impatient to insist on thorough testing of new ideas. Still, strong family and social connections ensured promotions for the British explorer.

On Scott's first expedition to the Antarctic one of his team members, Navy Engineer Lieutenant Reginald Skelton, suggested that motorized vehicles be used to travel toward the South Pole. For his second expedition, Scott asked Skelton to design and build a motor sled. Skelton agreed and, when it was built, shipped the sled to Norway for testing. Skelton, now promoted to Engineer Commander, joined Scott in Norway. The motor sled started, spewed smoke, and crawled across the snow for fifteen minutes before breaking down. Skelton's mechanics fixed the sled and started the motor again. The machine moved over the snow at the same speed that Amundsen could drive a dogsled. Scott declared that he had tested the machine enough. This was something Amundsen would in all likelihood not have done. The Norwegian would have tested the motor sled in different weather conditions and terrains, improving it until he was sure it would work.

The motor sled's performance that afternoon had satisfied Scott, who told *The Times* (June 2, 1910) "The motor sledge is a new development and bids fair to become the most promising means of polar transport. As a result of two years' experiments, a motor sledge has been evolved which has undergone satisfactory trials on the snows of Norway." Scott asked Skelton to build two more. The British explorer then made another mistake. He told Skelton that he could not go with the British Antarctic Expedition because, as a Commander, he would be senior to the person Scott had asked to be in charge of his ship. Again, Amundsen would probably not have done this. He would have found a way to take to Antarctica the man who had designed the motor sled so that changes could be made when problems developed. Scott did not seem worried about his new sleds "they are rugged...we will surely make it to the South Pole in ease and comfort. This is a new age of exploration and a new way of doing it."

In case the motor sleds didn't make it all the way to the South Pole, Scott planned to man–haul a number of wooden sleds. He didn't believe in the power of dogs because he had not been able to make huskies pull on his first expedition. He had said, "I am left in doubt as to whether we should not have done better without any dogs at all."

Amundsen was not surprised when he learned from Scott's writings that the British explorer had been unable to drive a dog team on his first expedition. It had taken Amundsen several years to learn how to do it. Amundsen wrote, "The dog must understand that he has to obey in everything, and the master must know how to make himself respected. If obedience is once established, I am convinced that the dog will be superior to all other draught animals over the long distances."

Scott was, in fact, taking a dog team and driver on his second expedition, in order to pull supplies as far as the mountains. Scott also took another animal that he preferred to dogs, but had never worked with: the Manchurian pony.

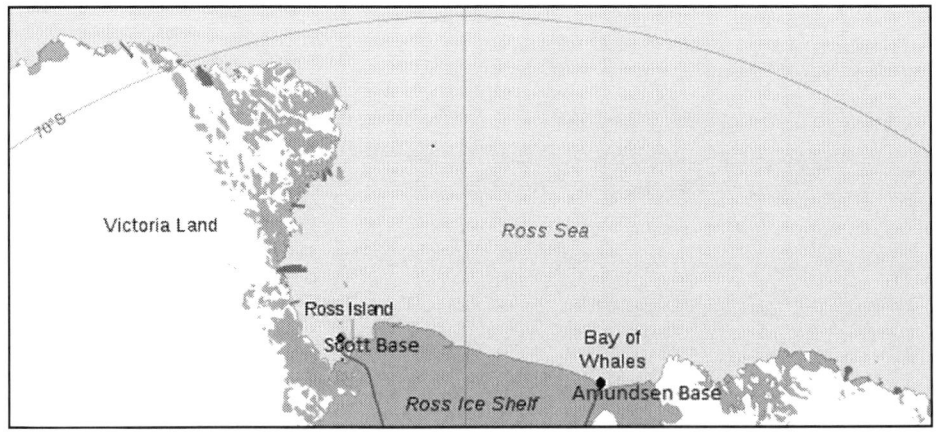

British and Norwegian Antarctic Bases

Back at the Bay of Whales, Amundsen invited the officers of Scott's ship, led by Lieutenant Campbell, to breakfast. The British returned the compliment by giving the Norwegians lunch on board their ship. Over the meal, Amundsen asked Campbell if the motor sleds were working. Campbell said, "One of them is already on terra firma." "Terra firma" meant land, and Campbell's comment made Amundsen think that a motor sled might already have crossed the Great Barrier and reached the mountain range. This was exactly what Campbell wanted Amundsen to think, but it was a clever lie. In any case, even if the motor sleds were working well, the British wouldn't be going to the South Pole yet. There was not enough time before the approaching winter. Trips had to be made to leave food and fuel in depots along the first part of the route for next summer's journey. And with the motor sleds, surely the British would easily be able to stock several depots before the sun went for its sleep below the horizon?

Amundsen in Pole Uniform

On February 10, 1911, with the Antarctic summer ending, Amundsen took four men, three sleds of supplies, and eighteen dogs over the Barrier to make a depot, so that on the following summer's trip to the South Pole the dogs would not have to pull a huge weight of supplies. One man skied in front, and the dogs followed. Amundsen marked the route with bamboo poles. The Norwegians built the first depot on February 14, after traveling 105 miles. With lightened sleds, it took two days to get back to Framheim. The *Fram* had just sailed for Buenos Aires to escape being trapped by the winter freeze, but the ship left a lifeboat in case the ice in the Bay of Whales calved and sent Amundsen's base drifting out to sea.

Norwegian Depot

On February 22, 1911, Amundsen and his men left on another depot trip with seven sleds and forty-two dogs. They traveled 175 miles, passing the first depot and setting up a second one on March 3. The temperature was 45 degrees below zero Fahrenheit, almost at the minus 50 degrees where Greenland huskies found it hard to work. The dogs' feet, soft from the long sea voyage, gave them trouble, yet Amundsen knew he had to build the food depots before winter, so he kept going for another 70 miles. He built the third depot on March 8. On the return journey, the dogs were so tired that Amundsen helped push a sled. He said, "I loved my dogs…I had asked more of them than they were capable of doing…I am naturally fond of all animals, and try to avoid hurting them."

By the time Amundsen returned to Framheim, eight of the dogs had died due to cold and heavy work. The sleds, made in Christiana, were too heavy and didn't pull straight. Six dogs had hauled 710 pounds per sled, the weight of four grown men, but 163 of those pounds had been the weight of the sled. Could Olav Bjaaland, the master carpenter, reduce the weight of each sled and re-make the runners so they pulled straight?

Amundsen also found that his ski boots were too small for the extra socks he wanted to wear to keep his feet warm. Perhaps Wisting, who had made shoes before, could re-make the men's boots?

Wisting's Workshop

The Norwegians made one more trip with supplies to the first depot before settling in for the winter. They saw the sun for the last time on April 19.

In spite of the eight that had died, there were still over one hundred huskies at Framheim, including puppies. Amundsen set up tents for the dogs.

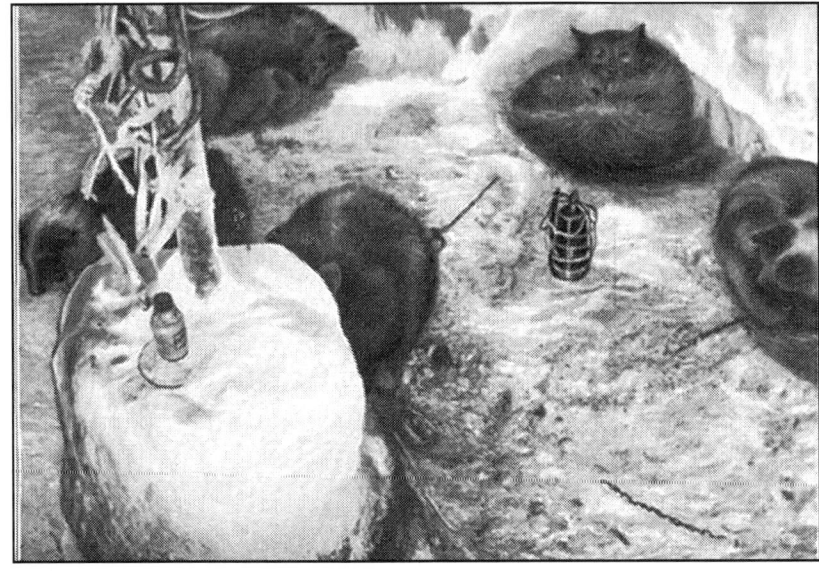

Dogs in Tent

It took two days to chip floors six feet into the ice to protect the huskies from wind. Each morning, the dogs were let loose. They would visit the puppies that preferred to sleep outside: balls of fur in the snow. Colonel spent each day with Suggen and Arne before Wisting chained him up again for an evening meal of either fresh seal meat or dried fish.

Suggen, Arne, and the Colonel.

During the Antarctic winter, while the tents outside the wooden hut glowed golden against the star-filled sky, Amundsen and his men worked on their equipment. Wisting made everyone's boots larger. Olav Bjaaland reduced the weight of the twelve foot long sleds by taking them apart, cutting and shaving the wood, then hammering and tying the pieces back together. When he had finished, the sleds were the same length and just as strong, but the weight was lowered from 163 pounds to 77. Bjaaland then did something else. Using the hickory wood that Amundsen had bought in Florida eleven years before, Bjaaland made three new sleds that each weighed 53 pounds, reducing even further the weight that a dog team would have to pull to the South Pole.

Framheim Work

The men worked hard, and Chef Lindstrom fed them well. On any given day, the smell of baking would waft from the kitchen. The men wolfed those superb hotcakes and washed them down with steaming coffee.

Lindström with the Buckwheat Cakes.

10

CROSSING
THE GREAT ICE BARRIER

Amundsen's mother may have thought of Roald as the *last* of the Vikings, but when on August 24, 1911, the sun appeared above the Barrier for the first time, the group of Norwegians who prepared to travel to the South Pole all had the hearts of Viking explorers beating in their chests.

The Norwegians wondered whether Scott had already left for the South Pole, but decided it would be too cold for the ponies. Then someone suggested the British might have started if it was warmer at McMurdo Sound than in the Bay of Whales. Amundsen said, "The uncertainty was worrying many of us…and personally, I felt it a great deal. I was determined to get away as soon as it was at all possible."

On September 7, the temperature was minus 7 Fahrenheit, well above the danger level of minus 50. The next day, Amundsen left for the South Pole. His plan was to travel in as straight a line as possible. On September 11, the temperature dropped to minus 68, and on the morning after that minus 62, with a breeze coming from the direction of the frigid Antarctic Plateau. Colonel, Suggen, and Arne lay shaking, with their noses under their tails. The men lifted the dogs and strapped on their sled harness. They started out, but Amundsen stopped traveling at ten in the morning and did what he had done the first time he tried to find the North Magnetic Pole: he built igloos to get warm. Then he did something else he'd done on that first trip in the North: he turned back, reaching Framheim on September 15.

Amundsen's best dog sled driver, Helmer Hanssen, took off his socks and said, "Why, I believe my heel's gone off!" The flesh looked like white fat and had a blister underneath. Amundsen cut into the blister. Fluid spurted. Hanssen said, "I began to fear that I should not be able to accompany the party to the Pole...But then Amundsen postponed the start for the Pole..." It must have been an enormous strain to wait and wonder how far the British had gone. More than a month passed before Amundsen could set out again: after Hanssen peeled away dead skin to reveal a fresh pink heel.

Helmer Hanssen

On October 19, the Norwegian team of Roald Amundsen, Helmer Hanssen, Oscar Wisting, Sverre Hassel, and Olav Bjaaland left on skis for the South Pole, with fifty-two dogs and four sleds.

Each sled pulled a wheel that was attached to a meter that measured the distance travelled. The wheel measurement could then be compared to measurements made by an instrument called a sextant, which navigators used to calculate position by sighting the location of the sun. Amundsen, Wisting, Hassel, and Hanssen were all trained navigators.

Hanssen drove first, followed by Bjaaland and Hassel. Wisting and Amundsen together guided the final sled, which was pulled by Colonel, Suggen, Arne and the rest of that dog team. After a day of travel, the men stopped and made camp. They unpacked the tent and drove in the pegs. Wisting slid inside and raised the pole, while the rest of the men tightened the ropes. Wisting came out, and Amundsen went in to set up sleeping bags, kit bags, cooker, and food. While the dogs were being fed, Amundsen lit the stove and filled the cooker with snow for drinking water. The men fed the huskies, a number of which had had trouble pulling that first day. Those dogs were let loose to return to Framheim.

A blizzard blew on the third day, the snow hitting Amundsen's eyes and whirling around the dogs, crusting their fur. Amundsen and Wisting kept blinking, trying to keep Hanssen's lead sled in sight. The Norwegians passed small crevasses and, to their surprise, no longer had to push their skis because they were gliding downhill. Amundsen had passed over some small cracks in the surface when, ahead, Bjaaland leaped from his sled as it tilted and fell over. The sled lay on its side, then began to sink out of sight, Bjaaland's huskies had stopped ahead of the sled, attached to it by the traces with which they pulled. The dogs had run along the edge of the crevasse, and perhaps disturbed the snow covering it. The sled was now pulling the dogs into the chasm. Bjaaland grabbed the harness, but the sled disappeared.

The ski champion slid as the wind howled. He yelled, "I can't hold it any longer."

Thirteen huskies lay on their stomachs, clawing the snow to save themselves from falling into the crevasse. Inch by inch, the dogs slid toward the crevasse. Amundsen and Wisting raced to Bjaaland. Colonel watched as Bjaaland's huskies whined, their legs stretched and paws scratching. The huskies closest to the sled slipped over the edge. Hanssen and Hassel turned like racing cars and charged back. They grabbed a rope and tied it to Bjaaland's sled harness. Amundsen and Bjaaland seized the rope, stuck their boots into the snow, and pulled.

The dogs stopped sliding. One by one, the men hauled the dangling huskies out.

Hassel ran along the crevasse, found where it narrowed, and pushed his nine-foot sled across the chasm. All the men hauled Bjaaland's sled up until it swung below Hassel's sled, to which they fastened it. Each man volunteered to slide into the crevasse. Amundsen chose Wisting. Amundsen and Bjaaland held Wisting's rope as he swung, untying and sending up box after box, including the food cooker.

Wisting looked at the bottom of the crevasse and yelled, "It doesn't look very inviting… immense spikes of ice sticking up everywhere…." After he finished, his teammates pulled Wisting out. His only comment was, "it was nice and warm down there."

The men pulled Bjaaland's sled up and reattached the huskies. When the sun came out, Amundsen found a path out of the crevasses.

The team took four days to travel the 105 miles to the first depot, reaching it on October 22. They stayed a few days, partly because of a snowstorm, and reached the third depot on November 2, having covered another 140 miles.

Before them lay a route that no one had traveled.

The huskies pulled the sleds over the Great Ice Barrier. The men left a snow beacon every 3 miles to guide them on their way home. Each beacon was made of blocks of snow standing six feet above the surface. Amundsen put a piece of paper in each beacon, telling the distance and direction to the one behind. The men also left a food depot every 70 miles. Amundsen wrote about how he marked each depot, "we foresaw that in a storm or fog we might easily get so far off our course as to make it difficult for us to locate a depot…we drew an imaginary east-and-west line through the depot and on this line set up flags on bamboo poles at intervals of approximately nine hundred yards, for a distance of about five miles on either side of the depot."

On October 29, the Queen Maud Mountains reared up from the coast where the Great Ice Barrier ended. The Vikings were about to climb into the mountains at a place 250 miles from Shackleton's route.

Amundsen was traveling 23 miles each day, at about the speed each hour of Scott's motor sleds.

Through
the Mountains

Amundsen wrote about why he thought he was a successful explorer, "A great part of my success in Arctic work came… from my hard-won apprenticeship to the actual life of the wilderness."

On November 15, the Norwegians built a food depot, marked it, and prepared to climb into the mountains. Amundsen was sticking with his plan to go in a straight line from Framheim to the Pole. He had traveled 385 miles. Another 683 miles stretched ahead to the Pole and back to the depot the Norwegians had just built. It was the distance from New York City to Indianapolis, Indiana.

Amundsen put 30 days of food in the depot and left 60 days worth on his four sleds. He needed to travel about 11 miles a day, far less than his speed over the Great Barrier. The route ahead, however, led through the mountains and across the Antarctic Plateau, which rested in deep cold at a height of 10,000 feet above sea level, about two miles up. Unlike Scott, the Norwegians would be forging a new route, so they didn't know what obstacles they would have to overcome.

Amundsen planned to take his remaining 42 dogs to the Plateau, kill 24 for fresh meat, and continue with three sleds and 18 dogs. The Norwegians would kill 6 more huskies on the way back. Hopefully, 12 dogs would return home. Fewer huskies would be needed to pull the lighter sleds back to Framheim because of the food waiting in the depots.

On November 17, Amundsen began the climb. The dogs trotted up until they reached a steep glacier. There, the men put the huskies into two 21-dog teams. Each team pulled one of the four sleds before returning to pull a second one. The Norwegians traveled 11.5 miles before pitching their five-man tent, after which Bjaaland put on his skis and climbed. The other men chatted until wood swished over snow. The ski champion slid to a stop and said he had found "the finest descent" on the other side. That night, Amundsen dreamed of mountains, precipices, and Bjaaland whizzing down from the sky. In the morning, four teams of dogs dug their claws into the snow and, step by step, pulled four sleds up to a mountain pass and through it to a terrace overlooking a valley. Below them, past some tongues of ice, the mighty Axel Heiberg Glacier rose in giant steps into another range of mountains and on up to the Antarctic Plateau.

Axel Heiberg Glacier

Leaving a beacon so they didn't miss the pass on their return journey, the Norwegians slid down to the valley with ropes wrapped as brakes around the sled runners. Mountains rose on every side. The snow in the valley was loose and deep, a powdery surface that stretched to small glaciers on the other side. Amundsen led the way for the dogs, breaking the trail on his skis just as he had learned to do when dog sledding from Gjoahaven. When he reached the steep glacial slopes, Amundsen asked Bjaaland to lead the way. The champion skied up a slope almost as steep as the side of a house, while after him the dogs double-teamed each sled. They reached a height of 4,550 feet, on a plateau in front of the Axel Heiberg Glacier. The snow was so deep that a tent pole could be pushed down and out of sight. The men trampled a place secure enough for the campsite.

The next day, Olav Bjaaland led the way up the glacier and around crevasses while the dogs double-teamed each sled, then raced over the flat parts. Snow spurted from Bjaaland's skis as he sprinted to stay ahead.

Amundsen worried about the altitude sickness that might come from working at these heights, because Shackleton had written about violent headaches on the 10,000 foot high Plateau. No one yet complained of headaches, or had trouble breathing. The Norwegians climbed until crevasse after deep crevasse blocked the way. They camped under a ridge at 5,560 feet altitude, halfway up to the Plateau.

Amundsen couldn't decide which way to go, so he climbed for a better view. To the right, ice lay jumbled against the base of a mountain that Amundsen called Mount Fridtjof Nansen. Ahead, the smooth side of another newly-named peak, Mount Don Pedro Christophersen, rose above ice crevasses that blocked the way to the next terrace on the Heiberg Glacier.

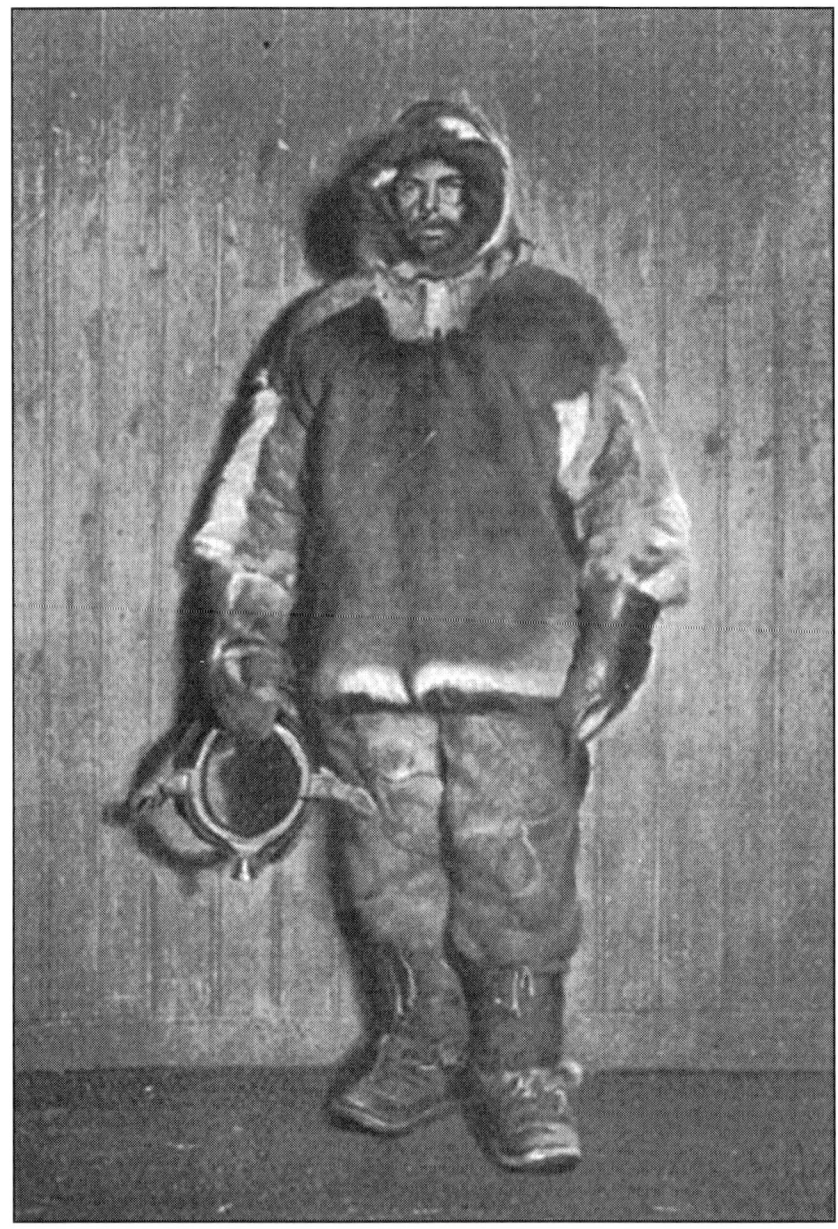

Olav Bjaaland

Amundsen studied the flank of Mount Don Pedro Christophersen and saw where the long even surface united with the glacier. The Norwegians had found their route. They sledded along the side of Don Pedro Christophersen and reached the next terrace, where they camped. The boom and roar of avalanches filled the valleys as the summer sun melted winter's mantle from the mountains.

Under the blue sky of November 20, Amundsen started out at 8 o'clock in the morning. Each dog team pulled a sled up the smooth surface of the glacier until it was time for lunch. The expedition stopped beneath the side of a mountain. Hanssen pumped the Primus cooker, lit it, put on the pot, added chunks of snow, and tapped in chocolate powder. The Norwegians sat, dressed in their overalls and underwear, sipping hot chocolate as ice crystals sparkled under the Antarctic sun.

Above them rose the steepest part of the glacier. Putting the stove away, Hanssen started the first sled. Behind, Colonel and his friends pulled Wisting's sled, their claws dug in, dragging their bellies up the snow. Steam streamed from Colonel's mouth as he stopped for a rest. Wisting called out, jerked the sled, and the dogs lurched forward again. All four teams reached the top of the Heiberg Glacier beside Mount Engelstad. Whiteness rose above them. The wind had pushed the snow into sastrugi waves that were hard as flint and sharp as knives. The drivers called out again, and the dogs leaned into their traces. Apart from yelling instructions, the men were quiet because they knew what had to happen next. The huskies needed fresh meat if some of them were to stay strong enough to reach the South Pole and get back home.

Amundsen made camp a full two miles above sea level, 10,920 feet, at the edge of the mountains looking south onto the Antarctic Plateau. The men hammered pegs into the hard snow. Amundsen went inside the tent and set up his Primus stove, hoping that pumping it to the high pressure needed to burn the fuel would cover the noise of what was to come. He wrote, "I was hoping thereby to produce enough noise to deaden the shots that I knew would soon be heard – twenty-four of our brave companions and faithful helpers were marked out for death. It was hard – but it had to be so. We had agreed to shrink from nothing in order to reach our goal. Each man was to kill his own dogs to the number that had been fixed."

Plateau Camp

The pemmican was bubbling when Amundsen jumped. "There went the first shot – I am not a nervous man, but I must admit that I gave a start. Shot now followed upon shot – they had an uncanny sound over the great plain. A trusty servant lost his life each time. It was long before the first man reported that he had finished."

Hanssen, Hassel, Wisting, and Bjaaland said goodbye to their faithful friends.

Amundsen wrote again, "The holiday humor that ought to have prevailed in the tent that evening – our first on the plateau – did not make its appearance; there was depression and sadness in the air – we had grown so fond of our dogs. The place was named the "Butcher's Shop." It had been arranged that we should stop here two days to rest and eat dog. There was more than one among us who at first would not hear of taking any part in this feast; but as time went by, and appetites became sharper, this view underwent a change, until, during the last few days before reaching the Butcher's Shop, we all thought and talked of nothing but dog cutlets, dog steaks, and the like. But on this first evening we put a restraint on ourselves; we thought we could not fall upon our four-footed friends and devour them before they had had time to grow cold."

Amundsen said (*The New York Times*, March 12, 1912), "what touched us most keenly on the whole journey was the unavoidable killing of dogs which had shared our dangers and done such splendid work. The killing of them went to the heart of every one."

That night, Amundsen turned slowly in his sleeping bag, trying to breathe at the high altitude to which his body was adapting. The men rested for two days, getting used to the heights, and regaining their strength after the climb through the mountains.

A snowstorm kept the expedition in the tent for another two days. On November 25, the wind howled, ice covered the tent, snow covered the sleds, and 18 well-fed huskies were curled together in a frosted mass. The Vikings had stayed too long. The British would be four days closer to the Pole.

It was time to get going.

Hassel left his Christiana-made sled leaning against the depot of fresh dog meat because the sled was no longer needed to carry food. It would make the depot easier to see on the return journey. At the last moment, Wisting stuck a broken ski into the snow as an extra marker. Amundsen didn't leave a line of flags, perhaps because he thought the mountains would make it easy to find the depot.

It was a mistake.

Harnesses attached six huskies to each of the three light Bjaaland-made sleds. Colonel, Arne, and Suggen leaned into their traces. The hickory runners slid straight. The Butcher's Shop disappeared behind.

Onwards To The Pole

12

The Race
to the South Pole

The New York Times (February 26, 1912) asked Robert Peary about the advantages of traveling with dogs versus ponies and motorized sleds. "I am old fogey enough," laughed the Admiral, "not to believe in a motor for arctic work, though it may work on the solid land of the South. But dogs, I think, are best. They are the only draught animal that can go everywhere a man can go. They are hardier than ponies. With their divided weight, they run over the loose snow of a crevice when a pony would be lost in it. They are smaller units, so that you can better afford to lose one. And, most important, when a dog dies he is food both for the remaining dogs and for the men. When a pony dies, the men can eat him, but the other ponies can't."

At first the ground rose, but then, to Amundsen's surprise, with snowflakes hitting his eyes, his skis dropped away. Bjaaland chased Wisting, while Wisting chased Hanssen. Amundsen shouted. Hanssen turned his sled to the side and stopped. After traveling twelve miles, the Norwegians made camp rather than risk falling into a crevasse in a storm.

The sun peeked out. In the distance ahead, the Devil's Glacier sparkled blue and white. Amundsen and his men traveled in fog and snow for several days, the sun poking through now and then to show the way. The men were ants between huge peaks that Amundsen named Mount Helmer Hanssen, Mount Oscar Wisting, Mount Sverre Hassel, and Mount Olav Bjaaland. On November 28, fog and snow blinded the path. Amundsen considered camping and waiting until the weather cleared. But, realizing that it might be a week before blue sky appeared, and worrying about where Scott was, the team kept going. That evening, Amundsen decided to lighten the loads before starting over the glacier. The men cut into snow that was hard as glass, and built a food depot that gleamed like a diamond. Sled loads lightened, they crept over the glacier, the fog parting now and then to reveal crevasses.

They traveled less than ten miles before camping.

On November 30, Amundsen wrote, "The glacier that day presented the worst confusion we had yet had to deal with." Ice hills steep as walls rose above crevasses deep as wells. Amundsen and Hassel led the way on their skis, a rope tied between them. A snow bridge the width of a sled hung over a crevasse. Like tightrope walkers above Niagara Falls, the Norwegians glided over the crevasse and into a long valley.

Snow Bridge On The Plateau

The team skied around ridges, moving back and forth as they traveled along the valley. The surface flattened. Snow filled crevasses. Ahead, huge domes towered. Amundsen climbed one.

The valley ice was smooth, but sprinkled with mounds the size of haystacks. Amundsen checked his compass and kept going south toward the Pole. By the end of the day, Hanssen's sled was sliding over ice. The men camped by knocking tent pegs into a milky-white surface. After setting up the Primus cooker, Hassel carried an axe over to a haycock to chip ice for drinking water. He swung. The blade crashed through like it was hitting a window. Ice tinkled into the abyss below. Hassel peered through the hole, brought his head out and said, "black as a sack; couldn't see any bottom."

On December 1, 1911, the Norwegian team headed into a blizzard that howled across the polished ice. Here and there, sastrugi gripped the sleds like glue. The men wrenched the runners forward as the huskies' claws scraped the surface. Wind cut into the left side of the men's faces. The temperature was minus 6 Fahrenheit. Amundsen made a depot and stored the reindeer skin clothing because it was too warm. Before them lay a polished-ice valley which the Norwegians named the Devil's Ballroom.

Hanssen led the way until his first dogs disappeared. He slid to a stop and gripped his sled, while Amundsen and the others raced up. They hauled on the traces, lifted the swaying dogs from the crevasse, and skied on until Bjaaland fell through the snow crust up to his waist. His skis hit a lower layer of hidden ice and broke through. The champion reached out, grabbed a loop of rope on his sled, and bent his arms and legs until his skis popped out of the crust and the dogs pulled the sled forward.

Time after time, dogs fell through the upper crust. Time after time, the men fell through, only to spread their skis and scramble out. The surface hardened and smoothed. The explorers headed south.

On December 4, the Norwegians traveled twenty-five miles, and the same distance again on December 5. The dogs were ravenous because they only had one pound of pemmican each day. One husky ate leather ski bindings; another husky ate a boot.

On December 7, when Amundsen was leading the way on his skis, shouts and cheers erupted. The great explorer stopped and turned. Tears ran down his face as Hanssen hoisted the Norwegian flag. Blue and red silk shone in a world of white. The Norwegians had passed the furthest point south reached by the British explorer Shackleton.

Amundsen wrote, "The tears forced their way to my eyes… Luckily I was some way in advance of the others, so that I had time to pull myself together before reaching my comrades…We did not pass that spot without according our highest tribute of admiration to the man, who – together with his gallant companions – had planted his country's flag so infinitely nearer to the goal than any of his pre-cursors. Sir Ernest Shackleton's name will always be written in the annals of Antarctic exploration in letters of fire."

The Norwegians, although 112 miles from the Pole, were about fifty miles over to the left of the spot where Shackleton turned around.

Amundsen packed 220 pounds of food into a depot, keeping thirty days of provisions on the sleds. Sixty pieces of wood stretched out as markers on either side of the depot. Amundsen did not want to miss the provisions on his way back.

The left sides of Amundsen and his men's faces were a mass of frost-sores from wind and snow. Puss floated on the wounds, while liquid seeped onto their skin. Each gust of wind cut like a knife into Amundsen's cheeks.

On December 9, the temperature was minus 18 degrees. The sun shone. Wind blew. Frost sores stung. Every step brought Amundsen closer to the Pole. The dogs lifted their noses and sniffed. What could they smell? Would the British flag fly above the Pole? Was Scott on his way back from the Pole after leaving McMurdo Sound with his motor sleds weeks before Hanssen's heel recovered from frost bite?

The Norwegians traveled for several days under blue skies and over crisp snow.

On December 14, they approached the South Pole. Hanssen wrote, "I thought the first one to set foot on the South Pole should be Amundsen himself…I stopped my dog-team and took one of the dogs out of the harness and let him run alongside. Then I called out to Amundsen to come on and run ahead.

"Why should I," he asked.

"I cannot make the dogs run without someone running ahead," I said."

Amundsen led the way on his skis. Hanssen looked for a British flag to flap above the frozen plain. Behind Hanssen's sled came Wisting, then Bjaaland. Hassel followed on skis.

Hanssen's neck stretched, his splendid eyes searching the horizon.

The plain was unbroken white.

Amundsen wrote:

"At three in the afternoon a simultaneous "Halt!" rang out from the drivers. They had carefully examined their sledge-meters, and they all showed the full distance – our Pole by reckoning. The goal was reached, the journey ended. I cannot say – though I know it would sound much more effective – that the object of my life was attained. That would be romancing rather too bare-facedly. I had better be honest and admit straight out that I have never known any man to be placed in such a diametrically opposite position to the goal of his desires as I was at that moment. The regions around the North Pole – well, yes, the North Pole itself – had attracted me from childhood, and here I was at the South Pole. Can anything more topsy-turvy be imagined?"

Hanssen wrote, "As always, Amundsen thought of his comrades, and when we planted the Norwegian flag on the South Pole, he made us each hold the bamboo flag-pole…"

Five frost-bitten Viking fists rammed the flag into the snow. Amundsen called the place Polheim.

Amundsen spoke, "Thus we plant thee, beloved flag, at the South Pole, and give to the plain on which it lies the name of King Haakon VII's Plateau."

Polheim

The Vikings stayed at Polheim for three days. Amundsen believed that the measured position of the South Pole was only accurate to within one mile, so he sent three skiers off in different directions for ten miles, where each placed a spare sled runner, a flag, and a note for Robert Scott should he arrive. While the men circled the camp, Amundsen made sextant observations of the sun and decided that the true South Pole was 5.5 miles away, within the area marked by the skiers. The group moved to this spot, and all four trained navigators made more sextant measurements. They determined that the South Pole was another 1.5 miles away, and that is where Amundsen left more pennants. He had triple checked the position of the Pole.

13
Scott

Robert Scott

Amundsen said the following about Scott, "Nobody could hold a higher admiration than myself for the gallant courage of our brave English competitors, for nobody else so well as we can understand the fearful dangers of the trip. Scott was a splendid sportsman as well as a great explorer."

Back on January 4, 1911, ten days before Amundsen reached the Bay of Whales, Scott had arrived at McMurdo Sound. Four days later, the British lowered one of their three motor sleds from the ship onto the ice. It broke that surface, dropped through the sea, and hit the bottom, coming to rest on the "terra firma" that Campbell, during the British visit to the Bay of Whales, had told Amundsen about.

Ponies at British Barrier Camp

Later in January, Scott set out over the Great Ice Barrier to build his first depot. Ponies and dogs pulled wooden sleds, which Scott had bought in Christiana, Norway, just as Amundsen had. Scott didn't take the motor sleds because they needed repairing. On February 3, after a day of plodding through deep snow, Scott wrote, "It is pathetic to see the ponies...Now and again one falls and lies trembling." Scott was experiencing for the first time how difficult it was for a pony to survive in an Arctic region.

On February 17, the ponies could no longer pull. Scott unloaded the sleds and called the place "One Ton Camp." It was the only depot Scott built before leaving the following summer, and it lay thirty five miles short of the spot the British had intended to reach. This decision to turn back early was one of many that combined to kill Scott and his team. All three of Amundsen's Barrier depots were closer to the South Pole than One Ton Camp.

Scott returned to find a letter from Lieutenant Campbell saying that Amundsen was established in the Bay of Whales. Scott showed his respect for Amundsen when he wrote in his diary, "There is no doubt that Amundsen's plan is a very serious menace to ours. He has a shorter distance to the Pole by 60 miles–I never thought he could have got so many dogs safely to the ice. His plan for running them seems excellent. But above and beyond all he can start his journey early in the season–an impossible condition with the ponies."

Scott did not use the winter to improve his equipment in the way the Norwegians did. Perhaps he didn't have anyone with the skills to re-make wooden sleds or re-design footwear. He certainly didn't have Reginald Skelton to re-design the motor sleds if critical weaknesses were found. When the sun appeared after the Antarctic night, Scott prepared for his journey. Unlike Amundsen, he didn't have to contend with a case of frostbite. It was stormy weather that delayed Scott's start, as did repairs to the motor sleds. On October 23, four days after Amundsen left for the second time, Scott wrote, "I don't know what to think of Amundsen's chances. If he gets to the Pole, it must be before we do, as he is bound to travel fast with dogs and pretty certain to start early."

On October 24, the motor sleds headed out over the Barrier. Scott set out a few days later, following the Shackleton route that led over the mountains to within 112 mile of the South Pole. The knowledge of this route was an advantage for Scott because, unlike Amundsen, he did not have to take the risks associated with heading into the unknown.

On November 4, Scott passed a broken motor sled. On November 6, Scott passed the second broken motor sled. He wrote, "Evidently the engines are not fitted for working in this climate."

The British continued across the Barrier; men, dogs, and ponies pulling wooden sleds. They reached One Ton Camp on November 15 and kept on going after a short rest. The ponies' feet sank deep into the snow. On November 25, Scott killed the first pony because it could no longer pull. The dogs feasted on pony meat. On November 28, Scott killed the second pony. On December 9, having run out of hay for the ponies, Scott had killed them all. The men feasted on pony meat, or "hooch," as they called it. The expedition reached the coast and prepared to follow Shackleton's route. Scott sent the dog team back to McMurdo Sound because he didn't think they could travel through the mountains. The British strapped harnesses over their shoulders and pulled their heavy Norwegian sleds through the snow. Scott said, "one sinks to the knee at every step." Each sled weighed 80 pounds more than the ones that Olav Bjaaland had re-made.

Man Hauling Camp 87th Parallel

On December 14, the day Amundsen reached the South Pole, Scott was in the mountains, clothes wet, lips blistered, and stomach cramped.

On January 16, 1912, a few miles from the South Pole, Scott saw something fluttering. He said "The worst has happened...it was a black flag...The Norwegians have forestalled us and are first to the Pole. It is a terrible disappointment."

British at the South Pole

Scott stayed at the Pole for a short time, verifying Amundsen's measurements and making use of some of the Norwegian expedition's leftover wood. Scott began his courageous return journey from the Pole on January 19, traveling about ten miles a day on little food, and writing one of the most moving journals in the history of the English language. Many were the mentions of the importance of eating the pony meat left in the depots. On February 18, near the Ross Sea one of the men, Evans, died from exhaustion and frostbite. The four remaining British explorers trudged over the Great Ice Barrier. On March 5, Scott wrote, "Regret to say going from bad to worse." A second man, Oates, had a frostbitten foot that blew up like a soccer ball. On either March 16 or 17, Oates left the tent, walked out into the blizzard, and did not return.

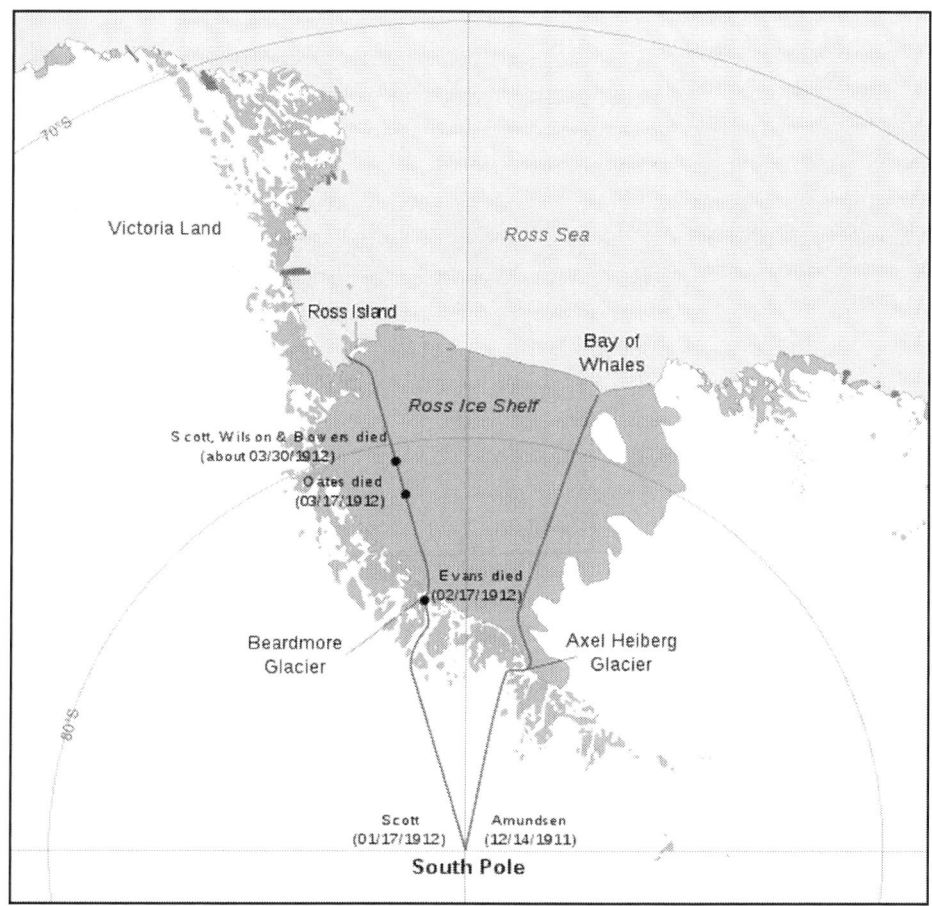

The Routes To The Pole

On March 20, eleven miles from One Ton Camp, weak from scurvy, exhausted from pulling, and blasted by a blizzard, the British companions crawled into their tent.

They did not come out.

Eight months later a search party found Scott, Wilson, and Bowers dead inside their sleeping bags.

Hanssen wrote, "What shall we say of Scott and his companions who were their own dogs? Anyone with any experience will take off his hat to Scott's achievement. I do not believe men ever have shown such endurance at any time, nor do I believe there ever will be men to equal it."

Scott's Grave

14
THE RETURN

Fridtjof Nansen said about Amundsen's conquering of the South Pole, "From first to last he and his companions have traversed entirely unknown regions on their ski, and there are not many expeditions in history that have brought under the foot of man so long a range of country hitherto unseen by human eye."

On December 18, 1911, Roald Amundsen, Sverre Hassel, Helmer Hanssen, Olav Bjaaland, and Oscar Wisting turned their backs to the wind and left Polheim. Amundsen wrote, "And so good-bye to Polheim. It was a solemn moment when we bared our heads and bade farewell to our home and our flag. And then the travelling tent was taken down and the sledges packed. Now the homeward journey was to begin – homeward, step by step, mile after mile, until the whole distance was accomplished. We drove at once into our old tracks and followed them. Many were the times we turned to send a last look to Polheim. The vaporous, white air set in again, and it was not long before the last of Polheim, our little flag, disappeared from view."

The path was easy to follow because the snow beacons shone like electric lighthouses or, when the sun shifted behind them, looked like black rocks. The team traveled with two sledges seventeen miles a day.

On December 24, the Vikings reached a depot, the contents of which they divided between the sledges. Wisting, the cook for the day, put biscuits into a bag and beat them. He added dried milk and snow water to make Christmas porridge.

Mountains came into view, and on December 30 the expedition neared Devil's Ballroom. Far in the distance, among the peaks, lay the Butcher's Shop and the way down over the Heiberg Glacier. Amundsen traveled around the glassy crust of the Ballroom. On January 1, 1912, the team avoided the huge ice hummocks and sharp ridges of Devil's Glacier to find themselves safe on the plain below. Here, they searched for the food depot. A fog rolled in. The Norwegians glided forward until the mist rolled away. Stopping on a ridge, Hanssen looked back and realized the depot was fifteen miles behind them. Hanssen wrote, "I said that if the weather stayed clear enough, I would undertake to drive back for it. Amundsen did not want to give the order, as he thought both men and dogs were tired. I said I would gladly go if someone would come with me."

Bjaaland volunteered to also go back. Snow spurted from under his skis as the Norwegian champion powered away. The world's best non-Eskimo dog driver followed with an empty sled. Ten hours later, Bjaaland and Hanssen returned with a loaded sled, having traveled thirty miles, for a total distance that day of fifty miles.

It was an incredible feat.

On January 3, after covering twenty-five miles Amundsen made camp at a beacon thirteen and a half miles from the Butcher's Shop. Several dogs had collapsed on the way back from the South Pole, and the others showed the same signs of exhaustion that Amundsen remembered in the huskies at Gjoahaven. He wrote, "This depot, which consisted of the finest, fresh dogs' flesh, was of immense importance to us…this food…had an extremely good effect on the dogs' state of health." Amundsen had only built two beacons during the bad weather after leaving the Butcher's Shop. Hanssen spotted them, but the sharp-eyed dog driver couldn't see the Butcher's Shop. The men passed one beacon and reached the second. Mountains filled the sky, peaks that hadn't been visible in the snowstorm as they headed toward the Pole. Amundsen wrote, "we were astonished at the appearance of the mountains…I would readily have taken my most solemn oath that I had never seen that landscape before in my life. We had now gone the full distance, and according to the beacons we had passed, we ought to be on the spot…we now only saw the side of a perfectly unknown mountain."

They should have left a line of flags.

Five pairs of eyes gazed at a cathedral of peaks. There looked to be no way through the walls of rock, and both men and dogs needed the depot meat if they were to have the energy to make it through the mountains on the path they had already travelled. Not finding the depot would mean death as the Vikings tried to find a route home while their dogs perished from starvation.

The Vikings were in trouble.

Yet, there was one among them with the sight of an eagle.

"Hullo," Hanssen exclaimed, "somebody has been here before."

Those splendid eyes had spotted Wisting's broken ski stuck above a mound of snow, in an ocean of white, three miles away. Amundsen wrote, "The most important point of our homeward journey had been reached…as soon as we had finished feeding the dogs…we set out."

The Norwegians attached rope brakes to their sled runners and left Butcher's Shop, steering down between the mountains and finding their depots along the trail of beacons. They reached the Ross Sea and headed over the Great Ice Barrier. On the flat ice the well-fed dogs stretched their legs. Amundsen decided that every second day they would travel 34 miles instead of just 17. The Norwegians moved across the barrier so fast, Bjaaland leading, that they didn't need all the food from the final depot that lay one hundred miles from the Bay of Whales.

On January 25, six days after Scott left the South Pole, Amundsen found Framheim resting safely above the icy cliffs of the Bay of Whales. Amundsen had been somewhat lucky. The ice at Bay of Whales did not rest on an island, or on the sea bottom, although it was protected by Roosevelt Island to the south. Significant calving of the bay's ice took place in 1955 and destroyed the site of Framheim.

On January 30, flags fluttered from the *Fram* as it eased away from the foot ice. On the decks lay thirty-nine dogs, many of which had tumbled around as puppies in the snows of Framheim. Eleven had been to the South Pole. Beside the main mast rested Colonel, with his two friends, Suggen and Arne, where they had stood for many a rainy day on the voyage south. Once again, Colonel howled when Oscar Wisting brought him food. In Amundsen's hand was a message from the Australian Antarctic Expedition asking if they could take over the huskies when Amundsen stopped in the port of Hobart, Australia. Amundsen decided to give away 21 of his dogs. When *Fram* left Hobart, Colonel and the 10 huskies that had stood at the Pole, plus 7 puppies, were still on board.

Oscar Wisting brought Colonel back home with him to Horten, Norway. The husky became well known to the townsfolk. When Colonel was in the mood, he would sit on the steps of the Salvation Army Mission and howl to the hymns. Colonel was so famous that after he died he was stuffed and put on display in Oslo's ski museum.

Amundsen was a hero. People in Norway flew the national flag. President Theodore Roosevelt sent a telegram, as did Peary who said, "Congratulations your great journey."

Fridtjof Nansen wrote to the *New York Times* and the *London Chronicle* that Amundsen's journey was "So grand – it could not be more magnificent. It is unique as a deed, as a voyage of discovery, and in its results."

On March 8, 1912, the *New York Times* reported, "It is thrilling news that the Norwegian explorer has overcome all obstacles and accomplished his purpose....this courageous explorer has risked his life and all the fortune he possessed in this great achievement."

In Britain, however, the reaction was different. *The Times* newspaper commented (March 9, 1912 "Captain Amundsen's Achievement") "From the telegrams now received there is little room for doubt that Captain Amundsen has reached the South Pole. From the English point of view he may not have "played the game"; we cannot forget the secrecy under which for months he shrouded his intention to steal a march on the man (*meaning Scott*) who had for years been making his preparations to attain the coveted goal. This was all the more unnecessary, for no one would have welcomed co-operation in the work of South Polar exploration more than Captain Scott. Unfortunately Captain Amundsen notified the latter of his intention too late for Captain Scott to get into communication with him. Still, no one who knows Captain Amundsen can have any doubt of his integrity, and since he states he has reached the Pole we are bound to believe him. For the present we have only the bare fact that he has done so; whether during his journey there and back he made any discoveries of importance we can only learn on publication of his narrative. One thing we know—he had nothing else in view save a "dash for the Pole." He had no intention of carrying out scientific investigations; he was unhampered with the heavy equipment required for this purpose; he had nothing to think of but his dogs, his sledges, his provisions, and clothing…(he) must have started much earlier than Scott in order to be able to get out so soon as he has done."

Whatever were the editors at the London *Times* thinking? What did "playing the game" mean? Playing whose game? Was it correct for the British to think that only they had the right to reach the South Pole from the Ross Sea? The first explorer to climb onto the barrier had been the Norwegian Carsten Borchgrevink. Amundsen had spent a winter in the Antarctic before Scott reached the continent for the first time. Should Amundsen have revealed his game plan to the man who had been quoted in the *New York Times* as saying "the south pole alone remains as our sphere of action. A race for it is certain in the immediate future."? What exactly should Amundsen have done differently? He was up against a competitor who led, in the words of the *Times* (March 9, 1912) "one of the best equipped scientific expeditions that ever undertook Polar exploration," and who's primary objective, per the *New York Times* (June 2, 1910) was not scientific exploration but being first at the South Pole: "Captain Scott admits that the main objective of his expedition is to reach the south pole and obtain for the British Empire the honor of that achievement."

Scott didn't encumber himself by man-hauling heavy scientific equipment. Neither did Amundsen, who notified the world of his intentions once he reached Madeira. He blazed his own trail to the South Pole rather than following the known Shackleton route that gave Scott the advantage of certainty.

As Fridtjof Nansen said about Amundsen and his Viking team, "They journeyed the whole time through unknown regions, and from first to last Amundsen found his way. It was considered certain in England that Amundsen would make for Beardmore Glacier, discovered by Shackleton, and by that route proceed to the high plateau, since he would be certain there of being able to advance. We, who know the man, did not consider this probable. It would be more like him to make his route away from the tracks traversed by others, and, fortunately, this surmise is found to be correct. At no single point to the pole itself does the route coincide with the English one."

As for scientific discoveries, Amundsen was an experienced geographer. Nansen commented, "Amundsen's many height measurements and observations during his journey across these glaciers and the inner plateau, combined with Shackleton's earlier observations, will be of the greatest importance in enabling us to understand conditions in this remarkable land..."

Once Scott's death was known, the British changed the description of his expedition to suggest that Scott's only objective had been scientific. Reports stated that he hadn't really been in a race for the pole. Sir Clements Markham, a president of the Royal Geographical Society, wrote the September 1913 introduction to Scott's Diary. In it Markham said, "Captain Scott's objects were strictly scientific… It was also part of Captain Scott's plan to reach the South Pole by a long and most arduous journey, but here again his intention was, if possible, to achieve scientific results on the way, especially hoping to discover fossils which would throw light on the former history of the great range of mountains which he had made known to science."

British schoolchildren were taught that Scott, not Amundsen, first reached the South Pole. Amundsen commented, "The year following the capture of the Pole, the son of a prominent Norwegian in London came home from his classes at an English school one evening, protesting to his father that he was being taught that Scott was the discoverer of the South Pole. On investigation, the boy's protest was found to be a fact, and the practice of ignoring the Norwegian success was being followed in other schools as well."

Amundsen attended a Royal Geographical Society dinner in London where the president, Lord Curzon, ended his speech by proposing three cheers for Amundsen's dogs, rather than toasting the explorer himself. This sneer suggested that Amundsen had had little to do with reaching the South Pole, but had merely been along for the ride. It also hinted at what had been widely criticized in England: the fact that Amundsen had killed and eaten many of his dogs. Lord Curzon must have forgotten that Scott himself had killed his dogs on the first British Antarctic Expedition, although Scott later changed his mind about this practice probably due to British public opinion and the fact that he had not learned to efficiently drive a dogsled. Furthermore, Scott had killed and eaten his ponies.

The British disrespect of his achievements stung Amundsen. He resigned his honorary Royal Geographical Society fellowship because of Lord Curzon's insult. Every man has his limit, and Amundsen had reached his when fifteen years later he wrote: "Scott was a splendid sportsman as well as a great explorer. I cannot, however, say as much for many of his countrymen...I feel justified in saying that by and large the British are a race of very bad losers."

Perhaps the last word should be given to the *New York Times*, to which Amundsen had granted the exclusive story of his South Pole expedition. Their article of March 10, 1912 said, "The first impression upon the reader of Capt. Amundsen's graphic but matter-of-fact and unemotional description of his conquest of the south pole is that the task was easily accomplished. But sober second thought removes that impression...From mid-October until late in January Amundsen and his men were toiling in the open. For more than three months, after an Antarctic Winter passed under shelter on the ice barrier, they were exposed to many changes of weather in temperature always far below the freezing point. From sea level they ascended mountains more than 10,000 feet high. The effect of this change of altitude upon ordinary men might be disastrous. These explorers were not only fearless and daring, they were men of extraordinary physical strength and endurance."

15

THE YEARS
FLY BY

Amundsen in 1913

It was several years before Amundsen continued with his plan to explore the Arctic Ocean. He wrote his two-volume book *The South Pole,* loaned money to Olav Bjaaland to start a ski factory, and traveled to America and other countries to talk about Antarctica.

While visiting Germany, Amundsen saw how in one hour an airplane could travel a distance it would take a dog sled days to cover. To learn more about this new form of transportation, Amundsen took flying lessons, then went for his exam at a Norwegian military camp. *The New York Times* reported on June 13, 1914, that an officer of the Norwegian Flying Corps took Amundsen on a preliminary flight around the course, "showing him what tests were required. Suddenly the elevator broke and the aeroplane fell, nose downward, to the ground, a distance of forty feet. Amundsen escaped unhurt, and the officer was only slightly bruised, but the aeroplane was completely wrecked. The explorer immediately afterward went up in another machine and carried out the tests required for a certificate." Amundsen had become the first non-military person in Norway to get a pilot's license.

Unfortunately, it was the same year that World War I started, and people no longer thought about polar expeditions. Amundsen still wanted to explore the Arctic Ocean. During the war, Amundsen made money in the shipping business in preparation for the time when he could start exploring again. *Fram* was too old to make another journey through ice, so Amundsen designed a new ship: one that improved on the lines of the *Fram*. He gave this design to a naval architect, who prepared working drawings and built the *Maud*.

In 1918, after the war, *Maud* left Norway. Helmer Hanssen and Oscar Wisting were on board with Amundsen. Sverre Hassel had returned to his job as a customs officer with the Norwegian government, and Olav Bjaaland was running his ski business. Amundsen steered around the outside of the Arctic Ocean and over the top of Russia. He was heading for Alaska, where he wanted to enter the pack ice and begin his drift across the top of the world. The ice was so thick along the Russian coast that it took *Maud* three years to reach Alaska, where a broken propeller forced the ship down to Seattle for repairs. Helmer Hanssen had to return to Norway, and by now Amundsen was out of money. The Norwegian Parliament gave their country's hero more cash.

Amundsen decided to add air exploration to the *Maud's* sea exploration, so he bought an airplane and took it to Alaska to try to become the first person to fly across the Arctic Ocean while Oscar Wisting sailed the *Maud* into the ice pack.

Amundsen fitted skis to his plane so that it could touch down on ice, but the left ski and part of the plane crumpled while landing after a test flight. To get more money, Amundsen went on a lecture tour of the United States, but he couldn't earn enough to keep the *Maud* sailing and to also repair the plane.

In November 1924, after a very slow drift in the pack ice, Oscar Wisting sent a wireless message to say that he had given up the attempt to make it across the polar basin.

Amundsen was broke.

While in a New York hotel in 1924, Amundsen's telephone rang. On the other end of the line was Lincoln Ellsworth, a millionaire American who said, "I might be able to supply some money for another expedition." Ellsworth wanted to team up with Amundsen and fly across the Arctic Ocean.

Arctic Region

Lincoln Ellsworth

Amundsen agreed and contacted Lieutenant Hjalmar Riiser-Larsen of the Norwegian Naval Air Force. Riiser-Larsen joined Amundsen's new expedition as a pilot and suggested that Ellsworth purchase two flying boats, called Dornier Do J seaplanes. Ellsworth did so.

Larsen also found out that an Italian airship, or dirigible, was for sale. Umberto Nobile, an officer in the Italian Military Air Service, had designed the airship and was also its pilot. Ellsworth began negotiations to buy the airship.

In 1925, Amundsen and Ellsworth took delivery of the two seaplanes near the town of Longyearbyen on the Norwegian island of Spitzbergen. Each plane had enough fuel to fly to the North Pole and back to Spitzbergen. Amundsen planned to land at the North Pole, refuel one plane from the other's half empty tank, and fly on to Alaska. This way, Amundsen would be the first person to reach the North Pole by airplane, and also the first to cross the Arctic Ocean, study the ice that covered it, and find out if there were any islands. It was a brilliant plan, since planes at that time could not quite carry the weight of fuel necessary to fly to the Pole and return.

The two flying boats were numbered N-24 and N-25. Six men went on the expedition: Amundsen, Ellsworth, Lieutenant Riiser-Larsen, another pilot, and two mechanics. Amundsen did not want to risk putting skis on the bottom of a plane again, so he would look for open water upon which to land. Amundsen flew in N-25 with Riiser Larsen, while Ellsworth flew in N-24.

N-25 near North Pole

After eight hours of flying, and thinking they had reached the North Pole, the pilots descended toward some channels of water.

While looking for a place to land, N-25 developed engine trouble. It came down fast, wings brushing an iceberg before it landed in a patch of water and stopped against ice. N-24 landed in a lagoon a few minutes later, hitting an ice floe before water gushed into the cabin. A navigational measurement showed that the planes had drifted during the flight and were about a hundred and fifty miles short of the Pole.

The water on which N-25 had landed soon froze over. Ellsworth and his two flight crew walked across to Amundsen's airplane and hauled it onto an ice block, where they repaired the engine. Now Amundsen faced the problem of how to take off again. Ice covered the water, and snow covered the ice. Amundsen had only 21 days of food for his men. There were no islands or animals in sight.

Around the world people wondered what had happened. Rescue missions were organized. Passengers on the Norwegian-American ship *Bergensfjord* (*New York Times* June 21, 1925) set sail for New York from an Oslo where prayers were being said in churches, and the city was in mourning because it was believed that Amundsen and his party were lost. Meanwhile, back in the Arctic, the expedition members decided to make a runway over the ice. They began shoveling snow.

At the same time, Amundsen took ocean depth soundings. He bored two holes in the ice, and lowered an underwater microphone into one. Into the other he dropped an explosive charge. One man fired the charge while another man listened on the microphone. The vibration of the explosion travelled to the ocean floor and then echoed back to the microphone after five seconds. This result indicated that the ocean was two miles deep, and that therefore there was no land nearby.

After twenty-four days of shoveling an amount of ice and snow equal to the weight of two hundred and sixty fully grown polar bears, a white surface stretched to a pool of water that led toward a twenty-foot hill of ice. Amundsen and the others stuffed themselves into N-25 for their only chance of escaping. They had just enough fuel for one take-off and, provided there were no strong headwinds, the trip back to Spitzbergen.

It was a life or death attempt.

Lieutenant Riiser-Larsen

Lieutenant Riiser-Larsen opened the throttle. The engine roared. The bottom of the flying boat crunched over ice and hard snow, rattling and swaying. Amundsen feared the plane would tip over and break a wing. The craft bumped its way to the end of the runway, leaped over the pool, and hit a cake of ice on the other side. With five seconds to go before crashing, Riiser-Larsen wrenched back on the control stick. The plane lifted and almost scraped the bottom of the fuselage as it cleared the hilltop.

The aircraft roared away.

With half an hour of fuel to spare, Spitzbergen came into view. A fault in the stabilizing rudder resulted in wind blowing the plane to the north of a cape where the men wanted to land. Riiser Larsen put the plane down onto the water. Twenty-eight hours later a patrol ship spotted N-25.

Two days before reaching New York, Captain Bull of the Norwegian-American ship *Bergensfjord* joined his passengers for dinner. The steward handed him a radio message. The Captain rose, ordered silence, and announced that Amundsen was safe. Cheers roared through the dining room. Champagne corks popped. Speeches and toasts to Amundsen filled the evening. William Nielson of St. Louis said he never saw such genuine joy at good news. All of Norway cheered Amundsen's return.

At the age of fifty-three, the Viking had achieved another triumph by reaching the Furthest North of any aircraft.

Amundsen and Ellsworth now contacted Umberto Nobile to see if the Italian dirigible was for sale so they could try again to be the first to fly to the North Pole. Nobile said that he represented the Italian government and would give Amundsen the airship if Amundsen agreed to fly the Italian flag. Amundsen refused. He was flying for Norway, not Italy, and instead negotiated a purchase price. He named the airship *Norge,* meaning Norway. Nobile agreed to join the mission as the pilot, along with five Italian mechanics. Amundsen asked Riiser-Larsen to also be a pilot and help navigate across the Arctic Ocean. Amundsen asked Oscar Wisting to be the officer in control of the *Norge's* main rudder.

Umberto Nobile landed the *Norge* on Spitzbergen for the next part of Amundsen and Ellsworth's exploration of the Arctic Ocean. The ship had an outside hull made of canvas stretched over metal tubes that surrounded several huge lighter-than-air gas bags. These bags lifted the dirigible off the ground. Three propeller engines and a control cabin hung underneath the ship.

The Norge

On May 9, 1926 the American explorer Captain Richard Byrd claimed that he had flown to the North Pole, having taken off from Spitzbergen in his airplane while Amundsen watched. Byrd had probably falsified his data, given that his plane's airspeed and fuel were insufficient to reach the Pole and return in the time he was in the air. Byrd knew this was his only chance, since Amundsen was preparing to leave. Amundsen could have left earlier than scheduled, but probably did not do so because he calculated that Byrd could not reach the Pole. Amundsen withheld criticism. The Norwegian now intended to be the first to fly over the North Pole and continue on across the entire Arctic Ocean.

Amundsen's cigar shaped airship, as long as a football field, rose above its Spitzbergen hangar on the morning of May 11 and flew out over the Arctic Ocean. In the evening, the *Norge* reached fog thick as a wall, rose, and flew over it. Riiser Larsen was in charge of calculating the course of the airship, using more sophisticated instruments than the sextant and sled wheels that Amundsen had used at the South Pole. At an hour past midnight, the sky cleared and the airship approached the North Pole. Riiser-Larsen knelt, checked the sun through a window in the gondola, and said, "Now we are there."

Amundsen turned and grasped Wisting's hand. They had become the first two people to reach both poles. Amundsen threw out the Norwegian flag, which dropped from the airship to the ice, followed by Ellsworth's Stars and Stripes. Nobile dropped armfuls of Italian flags, then produced an Italian flag so large that it had to be shoved out of the cabin window.

The *Norge* circled the Pole and headed for Alaska. At 8:30 in the morning, the airship again approached thick fog. Nobile was at the wheel, which he spun. The *Norge* rose until the gas bags inside the canvas hull expanded to the bursting point. Facing an explosion, Nobile turned the wheel the other way, but the nose of the *Norge* stayed up. Tears running down his face and hands shaking, Nobile screamed, "Run fast to the bow! Run fast to the bow!"

Umberto Nobile

Riiser-Larson took control of the *Norge*.

Men raced to the front. Their weight forced the bow down and into the fog, which created another problem. Water droplets froze, covering the canvas with ice that broke off, flew into the propellers, and made holes in the airship. The crew stopped one engine. Mechanics raced around patching holes, while Riiser-Larsen slowed the ship's speed so ice didn't fly off the hull like bullets. Instead, ice built up on the hull until the weight pulled the airship toward the ocean. Riiser-Larsen found a space between the fog and the clouds, and flew on. By evening the sky had cleared. At 6:45 the following morning, the crew sighted the Alaskan coast. They had been in the air 42 hours. Below them, open water lapped a coast where *Maud* had met impenetrable ice.

Once again, all of Norway cheered Amundsen's return. He had become the first to fly across the Arctic Ocean.

The New York Times (May 16, 1926) wrote, "Standing out easily today as the king of living explorers and adventurers, Captain Amundsen is a white-haired, ruddy man, with the hooked beak and quick piercing eye of an eagle. He is only 54 years old and is as spry as a cat, but twenty-three years of weathering in the Arctic have imprinted superficial marks of age on his face. It is spare and deeply lined. Hundreds of tiny wrinkles radiate from the corners of his eyes, the effect of years of constant squinting to protect his eyes from the Arctic glare…He is a Viking all over, a throwback to the heroes of the great sagas, to that amazing breed which, under the name of Vikings, Norsemen, Normans, and Danes, conquered their way over the world in the Dark Ages and early Middle Ages… He is a scholar and scientist. He is a plodding, careful geographer and cartographer, as well as a man of heroic adventure."

King Haakon and Queen Maud of Norway gave a dinner party in honor of Roald Amundsen and his comrades.

16
Farewell

At the age of 54, Amundsen bade farewell to exploration. Fridtjof Nansen said, "the greatest happiness is to be capable of the complete fulfillment of one's uniqueness...Such fulfillment you, Roald Amundsen, have achieved."

There was more drama to come, however.

In 1928, Umberto Nobile returned to the Arctic to fly his new airship, the *Italia*, to the North Pole. After the flight in the *Norge*, Amundsen had criticized Nobile for claiming too much credit for the achievement of flying across the Arctic Ocean. When the *Italia* disappeared soon after liftoff, the Italian government asked the Norwegian government for help, but the Italian dictator Mussolini withdrew that request and asked that Amundsen not be involved, presumably because of his quarrel with Nobile. The Norwegian government continued with the rescue operation because Nobile had probably gone down in Norwegian waters. The Norwegians made the rescue operation a military one under the command of Lieutenant Riiser-Larsen, thereby making sure that Amundsen, who was not an officer, could not be involved. Yet Amundsen wanted to help and had said publicly that he would do so. Many Norwegians thought it was disgraceful that their national hero could not rescue a fellow explorer.

While Amundsen was trying to find a way to help, Sverre Hassel came to visit him. Hassel was still a customs officer at the age of 51, and he fell dead while talking with his old leader.

A Norwegian businessman persuaded the French government to provide Amundsen with a plane. At the same time, radio contact was made with Nobile. He had crashed his airship near Spitzbergen and was, with a few survivors, floating on an ice floe.

There were at least twenty aircraft now searching for Nobile.

Amundsen's participation was wonderful but unnecessary.

Amundsen took off from northern Norway in a French Latham seaplane bound for Spitsbergen. Flying with Amundsen were a Norwegian pilot, a French pilot, and three more Frenchmen. The plane was overloaded, and Amundsen didn't return when expected. *The Times* reported on June 30 that fishermen had seen Amundsen's seaplane. "The machine was flying very low, the sea was rough, and the weather foggy."

Oscar Wisting led an expedition to find his leader. Lieutenant Hjalmar Riiser-Larsen also searched, as did many others, all believing that Amundsen would be waiting for them somewhere.

Amundsen was not seen again.

Months later wreckage was found. It consisted of the frame of an airplane and a float on which was inscribed "Latham Paris."

Helmer Hanssen wrote, "It was typical of Amundsen not to think of himself. I like to think that he met his death in the way he most wished to meet it: dying in the attempt to save others. In dying he lives and his name can never die."

On December 14, 1928, the country of Norway observed two minutes silence in memory of their hero. The *New York Times* reported, "All Norway paid tribute today to the memory of Captain Roald Amundsen who discovered the South Pole seventeen years ago today. Thousands of people assembled in the streets of Oslo and stood bareheaded for the two minutes of silence that was observed throughout the nation. The spectacle of the vast crowds recalled Armistice Day observations in other countries. Throughout Norway flags were at half staff and in the capital city more flags were seen than on any previous occasion in living memory. All day long, except during the two minutes of silence, church bells tolled from one end of the country to the other continuing until sundown…From almost every civilized nation the government received messages…A speech made by Lincoln Ellsworth in Brooklyn was broadcasted in translation by an Oslo radio station."

On September 4, 1928, *The Times* of London published its obituary of Roald Amundsen. The newspaper had not forgotten the lost race to the South Pole nor the assumed British right to explore in the Ross Sea area of Antarctica. Scott's incompetence was still ignored. Yet, *The Times* showed more respect for Amundsen than when it first received the news that he had reached the South Pole. Included in Amundsen's obituary was the following: "The great British expedition led by Captain Scott had left England the same year for the British sphere of exploration in the Antarctic, with the attainment of the South Pole as one of its chief objectives. When he reached Madeira, Amundsen announced to his party his intention to alter the destination of the voyage...When Amundsen's startling move became known in England some months later, there were many bitter comments on his stealthy intrusion into a field of Antarctic research which Britain had made peculiarly her own, and on the concealment of his intentions from Captain Scott, and charges of not "playing the game" were freely leveled against him. The personal issue assumed a secondary place to the brilliant success which Amundsen won."

In March, 1929, about eighty presidents of various national organizations signed a manifesto inviting Norwegians all over the world to subscribe to a Roald Amundsen Memorial Fund to promote geographical exploration.

In the 1930s, Oscar Wisting helped build a museum for the *Fram* in Oslo. In 1936, at the age of 65, Wisting asked if he might sleep on board the *Fram*. *The Times* reported (December 6, 1936), "Oscar Wisting was found dead yesterday on board the famous vessel of discovery, The Fram...He was highly esteemed by all who knew him, He was remarkably well qualified for polar expeditions, being a man of great versatility and practical skill." A Viking to the end, Wisting had died on his ship, just seven miles from the Ski Museum that housed his beloved dog, Colonel.

In 1956, Helmer Hanssen died at the age of 85. *The Times* (August 4, 1956) wrote about Hanssen that "Amundsen chose him for the voyage of the Gjoa, in which he surveyed the North Magnetic Pole and accomplished the North West Passage. Amundsen, who described him as the most efficient dogsledder he had met, gave him the leading sledge in the expedition to the South Pole. He also recorded that Hanssen had splendid eyesight and could spot tracks and other marks long before any other member of the party."

Olav Bjaaland died in 1961, aged 88, having lit the torch at the 1952 Olympics.

EPILOGUE

Who was the real Amundsen? Was he as underhanded as the British made out? Or was he a hero as most Americans believed?

Amundsen knew the shriek of the polar wind, the crunch of snow, the hiss of the primus, the thunder of avalanches, the groan of a ship's hull, the crack of rifles, and the cheers of success. He spent his life inspiring others with his leadership skills, attention to detail, determination, and joy in learning from different cultures. He compromised when he had to, prepared with excellence, led with inspiration, and usually refrained from criticizing others.

In the Arctic and the Antarctic, he went where no man had gone before.

In that September 4, 1928 obituary of Roald Amundsen, *The Times* also wrote the following: "He leaves a record unapproached in its range and its successes by that of any of his contemporaries in the same field, for to him belong the triple honours of being the first to make the North-West Passage by ship from end to end, the first to reach the South Pole, and joint leader in the first crossing of the North Polar Basin by air. If originality of conception was not his chief quality, his capacity for bold and resolute execution was unsurpassed. He was, moreover, a born leader of men."

Bibliography

Books

Amundsen, Roald. *My Life As An Explorer.* New York: Doubleday, Page and Company, 1927.

Amundsen, Roald. *The Northwest Passage.* London: Archibald Constable and Company Limited, 1908.

Amundsen, Roald. *The South Pole: An Account of the Norwegian Antarctic Expedition in the "Fram," 1910-1912.* London: John Murray, 1912.

Amundsen, Roald and Ellsworth, Lincoln. *First Crossing of the Polar Sea.* New York: George H. Doran Company, 1927.

Flaherty, Leo. *Roald Amundsen and the Quest for the South Pole.* New York: Chelsea House Publishers, 1992.

Hanssen, Helmer. *Voyages of a Modern Viking.* London: Routledge and Sons Ltd., 1936.

Huntford, Roland. *The Last Place on Earth.* New York: Atheneum, 1985. *

Kugelmass, J. Alvin. *Roald Amundsen: A Saga of the Polar Seas.* New York: Julian Messner, 1955.

Mason, Theodore K. *Two Against the Ice, Amundsen and Ellsworth.* New York: Dodd, Mead and Company, 1982.

Nansen, Fridtjof. *The First Crossing of Greenland.* London: Longman, Green, and Co., 1910.

Partridge, Bellamy. *The Splendid Norseman.* New York: Frederick A. Stokes Company, MCMXXIX

Scott, R.F. *Scott's Last Expedition. Being the Journals of Captain R. F. Scott.* Project Gutenberg.

Scott, Robert F. *The Voyage of the Discovery. Volumes 1 and 2.* London: Smith, Elder, and Co., 1905. New York: Charles Scribner's Sons, 1905

* Roland Huntford influenced me greatly with his fact-based views of Amundsen, especially in relation to Scott, but also in the last years of Amundsen's life. I have incorporated many of Huntford's opinions in my book, and the description of Amundsen's disappearance is largely taken from *The Last Place on Earth.*

Newspapers

New York Times. Dates of articles are cited in the text.

The Times. Dates of articles are cited in the text.

Photographs and Maps

All Roald Amundsen portraits, except "*Amundsen in Pole Uniform,*" are courtesy of *Wikipedia* Public Domain.

"*Nansen Crossing Greenland*" is from Nansen, Fridtjof: *The First Crossing of Greenland*, 277.

The following portrait photographs are courtesy of *Wikipedia* Public Domain: "*Fridtjof Nansen*," "*Sverre Hassel*," "*Helmer Hanssen*," "*Lincoln Ellsworth*," "*Lieutenant Riiser-Larsen*," and "*Umberto Nobile*."

The map on page 18 showing Hardangervidda is courtesy of *Traildino.com*.

All *Belgica* expedition photographs are courtesy of *Wikipedia* Public Domain.

"*The Gjoa*" is courtesy of *Wikipedia* Public Domain.

All Northwest Passage photographs, other than "*The Gjoa*," are courtesy of *Project Gutenberg*. Amundsen, Roald: *De Noordwestelijke Doorvaart*.

The Northwest Passage map on page 57 is from Amundsen, Roald: *The Northwest Passage*, Insert.

All Amundsen South Pole expedition photographs, including the dog photos in Chapter 7, are courtesy of *Project Gutenberg*. Amundsen, Roald: *Aan de Zuidpool*. Included are the following portrait photographs: "*Amundsen in Pole Uniform*," "*Lindstrom with the Buckwheat Cakes*," and "*Olav Bjaaland*."

All South Pole maps are courtesy of *Wikipedia* Public Domain.

"*Axel Heiberg Glacier*" is courtesy of *Wikipedia* Public Domain.

All Scott South Pole expedition photographs are courtesy of *Project Gutenberg*. Turleyaa, Charles: *The Voyages of Captain Scott*.

The "*Arctic Region*" map on page 145 is courtesy of *Wikipedia* Public Domain.

"*N-25 near North Pole*" is courtesy of *Wikipedia* Public Domain.

"*The Norge*" is courtesy of *Wikipedia* Public Domain.

Source Notes

The World in 1872
Page
5 "*How did I happen to become*": My Life as an Explorer, 1

Amundsen's Early Years
Page
9 "*Strangely enough the thing*": My Life as an Explorer, 2-3
13 "*Like all fond mothers*": My Life as an Explorer, 3-4

Crossing Hardangervidda
Page
17 "*I was ushered into an office*": My Life as an Explorer 4-5
18 "*involved dangers and hardships*": My Life as an Explorer, 5

First Man to Ski and to Sled in the Antarctic
Page
26 "*I simply had to see this ship*": Voyages of a Modern Viking 6
27 "*presents too great a surface*": The Last Place on Earth 68
28 "*It is certain that we honestly tried*": The Last Place on Earth 69
30 "*Within a week*": My Life as an Explorer 28
31 "*Gerlache knew for a certainty*": The South Pole Vol.1, 21

The Northwest Passage Part One
Page
35 "*My expedition must have*": My Life as an Explorer 33

36 *"Dr. Fridtjof Nansen"*: *My Life as an Explorer* 32
36 *"Young man, if you do"*: *My Life as an Explorer* 34
37 *"Roald Amundsen was going"*: *Voyages of a Modern Viking* 7-9
38 *"I besieged every possible source of funds"*: *My Life as an Explorer* 35-6
38 *"At last!"*: *My Life as an Explorer* 37
39 *"When dogs go loose"*: *Voyages of a Modern Viking* 16
39 *"We had no strict laws"*: *The Northwest Passage* Vol.1, 17
39 *"In the daily life"*: *Voyages of a Modern Viking* 16
41 *"If I had set a watch"*: *The Northwest Passage* Vol. 1, 70
42 *"No praise could be too much"*: *Voyages of a Modern Viking* 20

The Northwest Passage Part Two

Page
48 *"When we came right up to them"*: *Voyages of a Modern Viking* 26
50 *"the Eskimo dress in winter"*: *The Northwest Passage* Vol. 1, 149
55 *"All the Eskimos gathered"*: *Voyages of a Modern Viking* 61
55 *"We jumped, so to speak"*: *The Northwest Passage* Vol. 2, 107
55 *"I believe this was"*: *The Northwest Passage* Vol. 2, 116-7
55 *"We were in the midst"*: *The Northwest Passage* Vol. 2, 119
56 *"this was a significant day"*: *The Northwest Passage* Vol. 2, 120
56 *"My relief at having thus got clear"*: *The Northwest Passage* Vol.2, 123
56 *"I became conscious"*: *The Northwest Passage* Vol. 2, 125
58 *"An elderly man"*: *The Northwest Passage* Vol.2, 129

Planning for the North Pole

Page
61 *"The next exploit"*: *My Life as an Explorer* 64
64 *"It was in September, 1909"*: *The South Pole* Vol.1, 42
67 *"There is no real reason"*: *Voyage of the Discovery* 463
67 *"fifty pounds of edible food"*: *My Life as an Explorer* 70
69 *"Dogs first"*: *South Pole* 107

Heading to the South Pole

Page
75 *"The men who went"*: *The Splendid Norseman*, Introduction
75 *"He said he had deceived us"*: *Voyages of a Modern Viking* 88
76 *"informed regarding the experience"*: *My Life as an Explorer* 239

77 "*I had been greatly*": *My Life as an Explorer* 68
78 "*At first nothing at all happened*": *The South Pole* Vol.1 145
78 "*Before we let the dogs loose*": *The South Pole* Vol.1 147

Preparing to Leave for the Pole

Page
86 "*they are rugged*" : *Roald Amundsen: A Saga of the Polar Seas* 108
86 "*I am left in doubt*": *Voyage of the Discovery* 54
86 "*The dog must understand*": *The South Pole* Vol.1, 58
87 "*One of them is already on terra firma*": *The Last Place on Earth* 323
89 "*I loved my dogs*": *The South Pole* Vol.1, 238

Crossing the Great Ice Barrier

Page
95 "*The uncertainty was worrying*": *The South Pole* Vol.1, 379
95 "*Why, I believe my heel's gone off!*": *The South Pole* Vol.1, 386
96 "*I began to fear*": *Voyages of a Modern Viking* 102
97 "*I can't hold it any longer*": *The South Pole* Vol.2, 7
98 "*It doesn't look very inviting*": *The South Pole* Vol.2, 8
98 "*we foresaw that in a storm*": *My Life as an Explorer* 249

Through the Mountains

Page
103 "*A great part of my success*": *My Life as an Explorer* 238
107 "*I was hoping thereby*": *The South Pole* Vol.2, 62
108 "*There went the first shot*": *The South Pole* Vol.2, 63
108 "*The holiday humor*": *The South Pole* Vol.2, 63

The Race to the South Pole

Page
114 "*The glacier that day*": *The South Pole* Vol. 2, 92
115 "*black as a sack*": *The South Pole* Vol.2, 97
116 "*The tears forced their way*": *The South Pole* Vol.2, 114
116 "*I thought the first one*": *Voyages of a Modern Viking* 106
117 "*At three in the afternoon*": *The South Pole* Vol.2, 121
117 "*As always Amundsen thought*": *Voyages of a Modern Viking* 106
117 "*Thus we plant*": *The South Pole* Vol. 2, 122

Scott

Page
123 *"Nobody could hold"*: My Life as an Explorer 71
124 *"It is pathetic"*: Scott's Last Expedition, The Journals Feb.3
124 *"There is no doubt"*: Scott's Last Expedition, The Journals, Feb. 22
124 *"I don't know what to think"*: Scott's Last Expedition, The Journals, Oct.23
125 *"Evidently the engines are not fitted"*: Scott's Last Expedition, The Journals Nov.6
125 *"one sinks to the knee at every step"*: Scott's Last Expedition, The Journals Dec. 11
126 *"The worst had happened"*: Scott's Last Expedition, The Journals Jan.16
126 *"Regret to say"*: Scott's Last Expedition, The Journals March 5
127 *"What shall we say"*: Voyages of a Modern Viking 113

The Return

Page
131 *"From first to last"*: The South Pole, Introduction
131 *"And so goodbye to Polheim"*: The South Pole Vol.2, 134
132 *"I said that if"*: Voyages of a Modern Viking 111
132 *"This depot"*: The South Pole Vol.2, 151
132 *"we were astonished"*: The South Pole Vol.2 152-3
133 *"Hullo, somebody"*: The South Pole Vol.2 153
133 *"The most important point"*: The South Pole Vol. 2 154-5
136 *"The year following the capture of the Pole"*: My Life as an Explorer 72
137 *"Scott was a splendid sportsman"*: My Life as an Explorer 71

The Years Fly By

Page
144 *"I might be able to supply"*: My Life as an Explorer 120
151 *"Now we are there"*: First Crossing of the Polar Sea 141
151 *"Run fast to the bow"*: My Life as an Explorer 179

Farewell

Page
157 *"the greatest happiness"*: The Last Place on Earth 536
158 *"It was typical"*: Voyages of a Modern Viking 210

Index

Adelaide Peninsula, 42, 55
Adelie penguin, 83
Antarctic Plateau, 76, 95, 103, 104, 107
Amundsen, Leon, 18, 19, 20, 21, 52
Amundsen, Roald, vii, 10, 13
    as Second Mate, 28
    attempt to fly to North Pole, 147
    birth and early childhood, 3
    builds *Maud*, 144
    buys *Gjoa*, 36
    buys Inuit clothing, 50
    chooses Bay of Whales, 77
    climbs into Antarctic mountains, 103
    comment on de Gerlache, 31
    crossing Hardangervidda, 18-21
    death, 158
    decision to kill dogs, 67
    desire to explore, 5
    desire to be a captain, 17
    first Antarctic depot trip, 87
    first attempt at South Pole, 95
    first deception, 38
    first dogsled trip, 51-53
    first through Northwest Passage, 56
    first to ski in the Antarctic, 27
    gets pilot's license, 143
    gets *Fram*, 63
    gets scurvy, 29, 30
    hits reef, 40-42
    kills dogs, 108
    learns about Arctic equipment, 27
    learns to build an igloo, 51
    leaves Gjoahaven, 55
    leaves to rescue Umberto Nobile, 158
    lunches with British, 87
    meeting with Nansen, 36
    meeting with Neumayer, 36
    meets Inuit, 48
    near-sightedness, 17
    passes Master's Certificate, 35
    purchases airship *Norge*, 150
    purchases *Gjoa* and hires crew, 36-38
    proves Magnetic Pole moved, 53-55
    reaches Gjoahaven, 42

reaches North Pole, 151
reaches South Pole, 117
reaction to Peary reaching
   North Pole, 63, 64
second Antarctic depot trip, 88
second attempt at South
   Pole, 96
second deception, 65
start of de Gerlache
   expedition, 25, 26
talks to Ellsworth, 145
tells *Fram's* crew change of
   plans, 75
tells Hassel about change of
   plans, 71
visits stopping place of
   Franklin, 39
Astrup, Eivind, 10, 26, 50, 66
Arne (dog), 78, 90, 95, 97, 109, 134
Axel Heiberg Glacier, 104, 105,
   107, 132
Bay of Whales, 65, 77, 79, 83, 84,
   86, 88, 95, 123, 124, 133
Beardmore Glacier, 135
Beechy Island, 39
Belgica (ship), 26, 27, 28, 29, 30,
   31, 35, 37, 47, 51, 66, 84
Belgian Antarctic Expedition, 25
Bergensfjord (ship), 148, 149
Bjaaland, Olav, 63, 75, 77, 89,
   91, 96-98, 104-106, 108,
   109, 113, 115, 117, 125,
   131-133, 143, 144, 159
Borge, 3
Boothia Peninsula, 40, 53
Borchgrevink, Carstens, 65, 77, 135
Bowers, 127
Brabant Island, 27
British Antarctic Expedition, 67,
   85, 137
Buenos Aires, 88

Bull, Captain, 149
Butcher's Shop, 108, 109, 132, 133
Byrd, Richard, 151
Cape Colborne, 56
Campbell, Lieutenant, 86, 87,
   123, 124
Castberg, Sigrid, 62
Charles Hanson (ship), 58
Christiana, 3, 10, 18, 19, 37, 38,
   61, 62, 68, 89, 109, 124
Christiana University, 13, 50, 66
Christopherson, Don Pedro, 69
Colonel (dog), 67, 69, 70, 76-78,
   90, 95, 97, 107, 109, 133,
   134, 159
Columbus, 3
Cook, Frederick, vii, 26
   escaping the Antarctic ice, 31
   on Arctic equipment, 30
   on native clothing, 27, 50
   on scurvy, 29
Curzon, Lord, 136, 137
Custer, George Armstrong, 3
Devil's Ballroom, 115, 132
dogsled, 13, 47, 48, 50, 62, 65, 67,
   85, 137
Dornier seaplane, 146
Ellsworth, Lincoln, 144, 146, 158
Ericson, Leif, 3
Evans, 126
flying boats, 146, 147, 149, 158
Fram (ship), 62-64, 66-71, 75-79,
   83, 84, 88, 133, 134,
   143, 159
Framheim, 79, 83, 88-91, 95, 97,
   103, 133
Franklin, John, 9, 10, 20, 30, 35,
   39
Florida hickory, 35, 51, 91
Gerlache, Adrian de, 25, 26, 28,
   29, 30 31

Gerlache Strait, 27
Gjoa (ship), 36, 37, 38-42, 48, 52, 53, 54-56, 58, 61, 66, 79, 159
Gjoahaven, 42, 43, 47, 50, 53, 54, 66, 67, 79, 105, 132
Great Chicago Fire, 3
Greenland, 5, 10, 11, 26, 36, 38, 62, 66, 67, 68, 88
Haakon VII, King of Norway, 75, 153
Hansen, Godfred, 37, 41, 42, 47, 50, 51, 54, 55, 56
Hanssen, Helmer, 38, 48, 51, 52, 54, 66, 97, 107, 108, 113, 115-117, 131-133, 144
  on Amundsen, 26, 37, 39, 42, 117, 132, 158
  death, 159
  heel frostbite, 95-6
  on second Amundsen deception, 75
  on departure from Gjoahaven, 55
  on Scott, 127
Hardangervidda, 18, 19, 21, 52
Hassel, Sverre, 67-69, 71, 96-98, 108, 109, 114, 115, 117, 131, 144, 157
Hobart, 134
Holmenkollen Ski Festival, 63
hooch (pony meat), 125
husky (dog), 13, 27, 38, 39, 47, 51, 52, 54, 65, 67-71, 77, 78, 84, 86-91, 96, 97, 103-105, 107, 108, 115-117, 124, 125, 127, 132, 134-137, 143
igloo, 13, 49, 52, 54, 95, 13
Indianapolis, 103
Inuit, 10, 47, 49, 50, 51, 53, 54
Italia (airship), 157

Italian Military Air Service, 146
Latham seaplane, 158
Lecointe, Lieutenant, 28
Lindstrom, Adolf, 38, 48, 51, 66, 67, 69, 91, 92
Longyearbyen, 147
Lund, Anton, 37, 41, 48, 55
King Haakon VII Plateau, 117
King William Land, 42, 55
Madeira (island), 71, 75, 135, 159
Magnetic Pole, 35, 37, 40, 42, 47 51, 53, 55, 65, 95, 159
  theory, 25
  Amundsen's training, 36
  proof that it shifted, 54
Markham, Clements, 136
Maud, Queen of Norway, 153
Maud (ship), 144, 152
McMurdo Sound, 77, 95, 116, 123, 125
Mogen, 19, 21
motor sled, 65, 85-87, 99, 116, 123-125
Mount Don Pedro Christopherson, 105, 106
Mount Engelstad, 107
Mount Fridtjof Nansen, 105
Mount Helmer Hanssen, 113
Mount Olav Bjaaland, 113
Mount Oscar Wisting, 113
Mount Sverre Hassel, 113
Mount William, 27
Mussolini, 157
Nansen, Fridtjof, 10, 11, 12, 36, 37, 62, 75, 131, 134-136, 157
Neumayer, Professor, 36, 54
New York City, 103, 145, 148, 149
Niagara Falls, 114
Nobile, Umberto, 146, 150-152, 157, 158
Nordenskjold Islands, 55

Norge (airship), 150, 151, 152, 157
Norge (warship), 61
North Pole, 3, 25, 37, 61-64, 66, 71, 75, 117, 147, 150, 151, 157
Northwest Passage, 3, 9, 35, 36, 40, 42, 54, 56, 61, 65, 66
Norway, 3, 5, 13, 17, 18, 25, 35, 36, 37, 38, 39, 61, 62, 63, 67, 75, 84, 124, 134, 143, 144, 150, 153, 158
   dependent on Britain, 65-6
   testing ground for motor sleds, 85
Norwegian Flying Corps, 143
Norwegian Naval Air Force, 146
Norwegian Parliament, 144
Norwegian Society, 61
Oates, 126, 127
One Ton Camp, 124, 125, 127
Oslo, 3, 134, 148, 158, 159
Oslo Ski Museum, 134, 159
Partridge, Bellamy, 75
Peary, Robert, vii, 10, 26, 134
   on huskies, 66, 113
   reaches the North Pole, 62-64
Peel Strait, 40
Polheim, 117, 118, 131
pony, 86, 113, 124, 125, 126
primus cooker, 107, 115
Queen Maud's Sea, 55
Queen Maud Mountains, 98
Red, Eric the, 3
Riiser-Larsen, Hjalmar, 146, 147, 149, 150, 151, 152, 157, 158
Ristvedt, Peter, 18, 38, 40, 50, 51, 53, 54
Roosevelt, Theodore, vii, 61, 134
Roosevelt Island, 133
Ross, James, 35, 53, 65, 77
Ross Ice Shelf (Great Ice Barrier), 65 77, 98, 124, 126, 133

Royal Geographical Society, 136, 137
Salvation Army Mission, 134
Scott, Robert, vii, 49, 66, 76, 77, 95, 99, 103, 114, 118, 119, 121, 133
   on Peary reaching the North Pole, 64
   on use of dogs, 67
   on motor sledges, dogs, and ponies, 84-86
   newspaper reports 134-137, 158, 159
   trip to the South Pole, 123-128
Scott's Diary, 136
scurvy, 29-30, 39, 47, 51, 84, 127
Shackleton, Ernest, vii, 76, 77, 84, 99, 105, 116, 124, 125, 135, 136
Simpson Strait, 42, 54, 55
Skelton, Reginald, 85, 124
South Pole, 3, 25, 64-69, 71, 75-77, 84, 85, 87, 88, 91, 95, 96, 107, 116- 118, 124-126, 131-137, 151, 158, 159
Spitzbergen, 147, 148-151, 157
spontaneous combustion, 40
Suggen (dog), 78, 90, 95, 97, 109, 133
Teraiu, 51, 53
Victoria Strait, 56
Vinland, 3
Wellington Strait, 40, 53
Wiik, Gustav, 38, 54
Wilson, 127
Wisting, Oscar, 66, 69, 70, 89-91, 96-98, 107-109, 113, 117, 131, 133, 134, 144, 150, 151, 158, 159

AUTHOR BIOGRAPHY

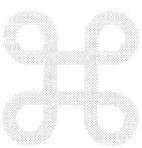

This is C.H. Colman's third book and first biography.
The Bald Eagle's View of American History was published in 2006.
Flaked Out: The Story of Cod and Newfoundland was published in 2011.
Charlie and his family live in Ohio and Ontario.

ACKNOWLEDGEMENT

The author wishes to thank the very helpful folk at CreateSpace.

Printed in Great Britain
by Amazon